Dancing As The Infinite

The Freedom of our True Self

Prasad

Master Peace Publishing
San Diego, California

Master Peace Publishing
P.O. Box 1063
Solana Beach CA 92075
Tel: 800-242-0363 ext. 2753
www.prasadsatsang.com

Copyright © 2002 by Prasad Foundation

First edition

Printed in Canada on recycled paper
Book & cover design by Chetna Bhatt
Back cover photograph of Prasad by Yolanda Pelayo
ISBN: 0-9719802-0-9

Library of Congress pre-assigned control number 2002093719

Acknowledgements

First of all I want to thank everyone who volunteered their time and energy to serve Satsang. There were so many of you, far too many to list, but please know that I carry you all in my heart wherever life takes me.

Thanks to all of you who transcribed the many hours of audio tapes and a special thanks to Saki Jaffe, Sally Hughes, Linda Evans and Santosh Deutman for your contribution to this book.

I am eternally grateful to Chetna Bhatt, whose grace and service to truth is endless, and whose beauty is reflected in the design of this book and to Amana Shebar, for your constant presence in Satsang. Every word is a reflection of our love and arose from the Silence that we are.

Om Shanti.

To
Ramana Maharshi
and
Papaji

Contents

Foreword

When I first met Prasad, his presence filled the room. His immense loving energy was immediately seen and felt, and his words pointed directly to Truth with an unusual and articulate clarity. In three years of travelling with Prasad, this never changed. Prasad's practical examples and contemporary metaphors serve to enrich a Westerner's understanding of the illusive experience of That which cannot be known, measured or named. Many of those attending his *satsang* gatherings have awakened to the Truth of who they are and that possibility exists for the reader as well. The words in this book exist for this. They arise from Emptiness, the pure Silence that is before, during and after words. In fact, these words were not written at all. Rather, they are from a collection of spontaneous public talks given throughout the United States in the final year of the 20th century.

Imagine a sonorous voice, deep and resonant, speaking to you as you read, and let the words fall over you as if they are the drops of a spring rain, and you are the river they are dissolving in. Then hear them, feel them, as if they are the river itself: sometimes flowing and fast, sometimes spilling over the banks of your mind, flooding reason. Sometimes you will hear the river negotiating sharp and sudden changes or turns, sometimes it is turbulent from a storm, sometimes you may hear the soft deep filling of long empty pools, and the "ahh" of resting there. Then, inevitably, you are thrown into the ocean. There you merge with these words, like the river does when it reaches the sea. You are in the ocean of Love, now, and the words are like ancient Sirens' songs, but they do not send you astray. They call you back to your pure and original nature when you have lost your way. Turn to these words when you need a moment's reminder of who you are and of the peace that is always present underneath your story or struggle. Allow them to instill in you the desire to be aware of the traps and pitfalls that the mind creates in separation from the innocence and purity of your true nature. Use them to remain vigilant to the simple unending truth: you are That for which you search.

This book was designed to be read in a number of ways. You can read each chapter from the beginning to its conclusion, or, you can open the book at random and see what message you have chosen for yourself. Or, you may discover that you can't put it down, and you make it one continuous read and then keep it close to you as a silent reminder of that which can not be spoken. However you use it, in these pages you can finish with the lie that the truth is outside of yourself, in someone else, in some other book, or in some other place. And, yes, in opening this book it is possible you may awaken from your endless cycle of suffering if you are available for it to end. These are the songs of your own heart. You hear them as you read them, and you know them intuitively as your own. You recognize them as what your heart has always known, as if they arise from within you. Allow them to reveal to you the Silence of your own true Self. Just place yourself in the river, and let it take you home.

Namaste,
Amana Aile Shebar

Enlightenment
is not
what you
Think

Before you begin reading this book, ask yourself, "Why?" Are you hoping to achieve something? Are you looking for something? For happiness, for love, for freedom? Well, this very search is all that keeps you from recognizing the truth: you are already That which you seek! You can look anywhere and everywhere you want to. You can follow any and every path you feel drawn to, but none of it will take you to the truth of who you are. It is all postponement, for you are already That; this is why we gather in satsang, to realize what is already so. Satsang is not a path, it is not a process, it is not an organization, and it certainly is not a religion! It is simply gathering together and being available to the truth of who you are. Satsang literally means a gathering in truth, and it is different from most spiritual gatherings. Instead of perceiving yourself as somebody who has to achieve something—through whatever path or practice or austerities are being imposed on you—you are recognized in satsang as already That. You don't come to get anything; you don't come to attain anything; you don't come to understand anything. You come to recognize that you are already free; you cannot be otherwise.

If you have any concepts about enlightenment, let them be burned at the stake! If you have any idea about what you have to do first, how long you have to practice for, what you have to attain, what it will look like, whether it is fits of ecstasy or unending bliss—whatever your story about enlightenment is, drop it! Whatever you believe heaven or nirvana to be, as sacred as your beliefs may be, surrender them. Surrender whatever is in your way of realizing who you are here and now, in this nothingness, in this no-thing-ness. Concept-free, thought-less, empty, pure, vast, infinite, and endless like the sky.

Enlightenment is not a becoming. You don't become enlightened. You're not at one point ignorant and then, the next moment, enlightened. This is all mind. You already are That. It's a simple realization that happens by dropping everything else you believe about yourself. Drop all your beliefs and see what happens. Drop your point of view and see what remains. Drop your proverbial pursuit of happiness. Stop chasing your desires, stop running from your fears; stop everything, right now, and see what is so, what does not come and go— what simply is, regardless of what you feel about it, or what you think about it. Your thoughts, your feelings, your physical sensations cannot touch this absolute Self that you are, so why give them so much credence? Why give them so much importance? They are phantoms; they are written on the wind.

Enlightenment is not what you think. Enlightenment is ordinary. It's been deified for so long, made so rare, so special, that everybody who wants to be special chases it. You want to be special so you chase enlightenment, and then, if it shows up to be ordinary, you say, "I don't want that! It's ordinary; I'm looking for something mystical and magical. The fireworks haven't gone off yet." Forget about the extraordinary; all of those mystical and magical states are temporary. They are symptoms of freedom and they come and go. Freedom is your natural state, and it is eternal. See it as ordinary. It's not rare—you make it rare. It's not special—you make it special. Anyone who thinks enlightenment is something special will never realize it, because enlightenment happens to nobody. If you want to be special, if you want to be somebody, then your whole pursuit of enlightenment keeps this somebody alive. When you're ripe for realization, you are ripe to let go of your identification with somebody. Realization happens to nobody.

Stop trying to be somebody; stop trying to become something. There is no becoming; you already are. Becoming is mind. In freedom you already are; you can not be otherwise. Recognize this truth and then set yourself free to be whatever it is that shows up in the moment. Stop trying to be something that your mind tells you to be or not to be. Do not doubt; remove doubt and see freedom as ordinary. Drop this whole myth of enlightenment being for just the selected few! This is such bunk; this is not truth. Enlightenment is ordinary! You don't have to be special, some swami, or some saint to recognize the truth. Enlightenment is ordinary, if you just stop believing in the dream. Then it's so obvious that there's nobody to wake up. Nobody wakes up— only somebody was asleep, but nobody wakes up. Finish with this somebody with all his silly ideas about enlightenment. Put an end to somebody. Be nobody.

The truth does not come and go, and it does not appear and disappear. It is constant and is not based in duality. The truth has nothing to do with what you believe or disbelieve, so it's irrelevant whether you agree or disagree. Let me be clear. I'm not asking you to surrender your beliefs in exchange for mine. I'm just asking you to surrender your beliefs. In that moment you see the truth for yourself. That's why it's not relevant whether you believe or don't believe in what I am saying on the absolute level. Realize yourself as the absolute, and then everything you believe is seen in the proper perspective. It's seen as temporary, as ephemeral, as meaningless. It comes and goes. You don't rely on it; you don't depend on it. As quickly as it rises, it falls again, but it doesn't touch you. Can you let go of your beliefs for one second to realize this truth, here and now?

If you think you'll no longer have sadness or anger or fear in enlightenment, then you better be willing also to give up joy, happiness, and laughter. As long as you have happiness, you have unhappiness. As long as you have joy, you have sadness; as long as you have peace, you have anger. They go hand in hand. Celebrate your emotions; it's part of being alive in these bodies! Don't be afraid of them; only the mind judges this emotion as bad and that emotion as good. It's just a conditioned response to dislike your tears. It feels fantastic to let yourself weep and sob. It's like a really good monsoon! It's fantastic to let yourself rage like lightning and thunder! Don't be afraid of your feelings; it's all just weather. The clouds are coming, the rain is coming, the sun is coming, but nobody judges the weather. Just accept that this is the weather; you may not like it, but what can you do? You accept it; you don't try to change it. How can you change the weather? Even if you don't like it, how can you change it? And when you are out of the way, when you are still, when you are not chasing your thoughts, when you are simply watching them—you see that anger is exactly the same as laughter. It's all just energy expressing itself.

In freedom, every moment is blissful. Even when you seem to be angry and upset, you still remain blissful. Haven't you ever thrown a good temper tantrum? Doesn't it feel great? Haven't you ever cried at a movie? Doesn't it feel wonderful? Just watch your emotions rise and fall. See them do their dance and not touch you. The more open you are, the more you'll feel, but in truth, they're just feelings. They're not important. The moment you feel them they're already past. The minute you say it, it's already a lie—this is why the truth cannot be spoken. This is why I cannot tell you what is true. You can only realize truth for yourself in the stillness of silence. So give up everything. Give up everything and be still. When you are sitting still, not chasing your mind or avoiding your feelings, then truth is available. Be available to it, and you will see what has been here all along, the pure Awareness of your own Self. It doesn't matter what the circumstances of your life are, whether you are with your family, whether you are alone, whether you are at work or at play. It doesn't matter, because you are always with your own Self. This is the constant that you can depend on, this silence, this love, this oneness. Then every time the "I" rises, you don't have to believe it.

The "I" is the source of all suffering. The "I" is the separation. This poor "I" has been trying to reconnect with God in every imaginable way for ages, and the truth is, it already is one with God! It rises from God and returns to God in each moment. It is never separate from God. Yet this "I" has been struggling to return to God for lifetimes: meditating, doing workshops, and practicing yoga; searching for it in relationship, trying to merge through lovemaking, looking for it in drugs and sex and rock and roll; looking for it in material success through some outer manifestation of approval. The more you chase it, the further away the experience of love is. So I am here to tell you: stop! Let go. Be still and you will realize everything you ever wanted is right here. You already are It. And once you realize it, then you resume your life in a rich and ordinary way.

It's very ordinary to wake up and realize yourself. It's very ordinary because it's your natural state. It's who you are. What's extraordinary is being willing to stop your seeking. Be willing to say, "This is it, this moment is it."Doubt rises: "This can't be it. Impossible! It can't be this easy." This is why enlightened masters like the Buddha, Ramana Maharshi, and Papaji are honored, because they dropped the doubt. They said, "Enough. This is it. I am That, and nothing can take me from this realization. Nothing." To abide in it, to live eternally in this freedom—that's what's available when you stop seeking. Seeking comes from doubting. If you're still seeking somewhere, stop! When your doubt creeps in again, you must be vigilant. Don't let it! It's just a thought; it's a trick of the mind. You are free. Now live from this truth and don't believe anything else. Believe only That and let all the rest come and go.

Make freedom your master. Make truth the focus of your life. Then it's easy to be vigilant. But let something else distract you, let something else be more important, and you find yourself off and running again, once more seeking, once more doubting, once more fearing, once more suffering. All of that is so unnecessary at this point in your evolvement. Be uninvolved and you are evolved. Don't get so involved in your lives. They come and they go; they're not important. This moment is all that's important. This moment is all that exists. Be available to this moment and it's available to you. Everything else takes care of itself, moment by moment. No doubt rises, no fear rises, nothing rises that can take you out of this realization.

When you wake up, your whole life, which is based on a lie, will fall away—and your life will be seen clearly for what it is. You won't be able to hide in ignorance any longer, as much as you try. As you continue to awaken, the suffering may seem more intense for a while, because you become more aware of the suffering that is already present. People run away from it. They don't want to face it, but it's just part of awakening from the dream. When you let go of the lie, you have nothing. It's that one moment of letting go of the lie—the misidentification with your life as real, the misidentification with your point of view called "me"—that shakes you out of your slumber, that cracks open the veil. You begin to question. Then you begin to see the truth. This is a definitive moment. The mind will try to resist with its old stories and defenses, but that's the moment to be still, to keep quiet, not to touch the story no matter what. Do not listen to your mind, no matter what it tells you. Simply keep still.

There is a saying, "Before enlightenment, chop wood and carry water. After enlightenment, chop wood and carry water," but when you are carrying the water it's a whole different ballgame! Suddenly, while carrying the water you are dancing; suddenly, while chopping the wood you're one with the ax and the log. Each moment becomes a celebration. Old behavior falls away if it was ego-driven. Old habits and misidentification and relationships either go away or upgrade themselves. Desire may burn up; fear may disappear, but definitely, whoever it was who was suffering is nowhere to be found. There is no longer somebody to suffer or doubt or seek. The beauty of this is, it happens all by itself, just like the rose blossoming. You can't do anything to make a rose blossom. You just sit and watch the unfolding.

What is enlightenment, really? It's just a concept. You don't know what it is to be enlightened, but you do know what it is to be happy. It's our natural state; we've all been happy. So we come to satsang to learn how to be unconditionally happy, happy all the time, happy regardless of the circumstances of our lives, regardless of what's happening emotionally or physically. This is the natural state of happiness, the unconditional happiness that never comes and never goes, that constant state of bliss that we rest in while we watch our lives go by. Physical sensations may be challenging: some pain, some aging, some disease; emotional reactions may be challenging: anger, sadness, fear, guilt, shame. It all comes and goes, but it doesn't touch your happiness. Once you've recognized this happiness that you are, it doesn't go away. You abide here in the happiness. Like the enlightened mystic Meher Baba used to say, "Don't worry, be happy." If you could crystallize what it is to be enlightened, you could crystallize it into that one sentence. Mind is worry. No-mind is happy.

Be happy with who you are this lifetime. Whoever it is, be happy with it! You know who you are in form: your bodies are changing, your minds are constantly changing, your emotions are changing. You know this. This is who you are in form. Be happy with it, because it's changing anyway. If you don't like it, it will change! If you like it, it will change! Be happy and watch these movies of your life rise and fall. Be happy with the challenges. Be happy with the hard times; be happy with the easy times. Be happy with whatever shows up in your life. Accept whatever is—don't mind your mind. I'm not telling your minds to be happy; minds are only happy when they get what they want, like a dog. They wag their tail when they get it, and they beg when they don't! They bark when they're afraid, or they run away. These are minds. Minds are dogs! I'm speaking to you, not your minds. Be happy with your creation. Be happy that you are here now, and always be here now! When you're happy, you're not seeking anymore. You're not working on yourself anymore. You're just living your life, allowing your life to reveal itself moment by moment, trusting that whatever shows up is perfect.

Happiness happens not because your desire is fulfilled, but because in that moment there is no desire. Do you understand? In that moment when desire is fulfilled, it appears that you are happy because there is no desire. Freedom is desirelessness—and all desire, including the desire for freedom, takes you out of freedom. So have no desires, just let them come and go. Neither indulge in them nor repress them. Just let them be. Don't be afraid of desire, but be the master of desire. Don't let your desires run you. See clearly that the desireless state is freedom. Desire nothing and let Existence give to you. Simply say "yes" to whatever is, and it's easy to live in freedom. Say "yes" to whatever comes, and "yes" when it goes. Welcome, and goodbye. Easy come, easy go. If you let go of desire, then happiness always is.

To think that every time you have a desire for something, you have to fulfill it—this is the mind. In truth, desires rise and fall all the time. Some of them fulfill themselves, and some of them don't. This is freedom! Let them come and go. Sometimes they go; sometimes they come. Let them come and go. Don't you do them. There's nothing wrong with desires. It's the misidentification with them and the attachment to them being fulfilled that causes all the suffering. There's nothing wrong with sex; it's thinking about it all the time that's the problem! Don't be a whore to your desires. Your suffering never has to do with the other. It's always your own story that's creating the suffering. Whenever there is suffering, inquire, "Who's suffering?" Whenever there is desire, inquire, "Who wants?" Shine the light on yourself. See what your story is and drop it as fast as you can for stories will rise and try to distract you and vie for your attention. Don't give in to them. Neglect your story until it withers away and dies.

It's easy to be free, while your ego is getting its way, while your life is flowing and going well, you won't even notice your story. It will feel like freedom. You have a new lover, you've built a new house, you love your job, life is flowing. You're happy. But ask yourself, "Who is happy?" Take away the conditions of your life and see if the happiness remains. If you haven't seen that this ego is not who you are, you will suffer. And in that moment of suffering it will appear as if your awakening was just a load of bunk. It's easy to feel free when the ego is getting what it wants, but what happens when the ego doesn't get what it wants? It immediately goes into its routines, like when the ego meets fear, it immediately goes into fight or flight. But if you're aware of these tendencies, if you know them well, then you see them and you don't have to act on them, you simply witness them. "There's my tendency, there's my story, I don't have to go there, because it's not who I am. This tendency has risen and by watching it, it doesn't grab hold of me." But if you pretend you don't have these impulses, these desires, these fears, these aversions, then they've got you.

If you're living your life to get your desires met, you're living a shallow life. It's an ego-driven life, and it's hit or miss at best. Sometimes the desires are fulfilled and you feel happy, sometimes they're not and you feel miserable. It's like betting the horses. Some of you have good odds, some of you have better than good odds, and some of you have terrible odds. What to do? It's called *karma*. But if you choose to stop the race, to stop betting, you can transcend your karma. It means the horses keep running but you've got no money on the race, so who cares? Who cares if the horse wins or not; you've got nothing at stake. Do this with your own lives! Then you can enjoy the race; you can cheer the horses on. There's nobody who's invested; there's nobody who cares. Try it and see. Live your life as if it's somebody else's. Don't take anything personally.

When your desires rise, give permission to them. Don't resist them, don't say "no," but don't engage in them either. Don't make it important that the desire fulfill itself. If you do, you are a beggar, begging for quarters, waiting for that big jackpot that never seems to come. And if one day it comes, what happens immediately after? More and more quarters. It lasts a split second. You put in your quarter, you pull the one-armed bandit, and then you get some quarters back. See, I got what I wanted! Put in more quarters, more quarters: pull, pull, pull. You think your happiness has something to do with the fact that you're putting in quarters and getting quarters back. You think your happiness is related to the desires coming true, and all that happens in the moment is you let go of your desire. In that moment when the quarters come down you feel rich. But those are the quarters you've just put in the machine! You've just been spending an hour putting $300 worth of quarters in the machine, and now you get them back and you feel good! When you let go of desires and live in the ease of desirelessness, even though you have a lot of quarters, there may be no desire to play the slot machine. You may walk by and say to yourself, "I have my quarters, but I don't need to put them in the machine today. Maybe I'll give them away instead."

In truth, underneath every desire that rises is a desire for peace. Look for yourselves. Everything you desire: success in your relationships, in your career, in your health and wealth, it's all the same desire. It's all a longing to be at peace. When you stop seeking it in the fleeting objects of desire and keep still, peace is realized as already present. It never leaves you. You only leave it in search of peace. So stay home and be at peace. When you stop chasing your desires, you become wise, and you see that everything is available. You don't have to chase it. Be available and it comes to you. The chasing makes you a pauper, a beggar. Sit still and you are the king, you are the queen—everything is available to you in this stillness. Trust Existence that whatever is happening in that moment is perfect, no matter what your mind tells you. Stop looking outside yourself and be finished.

When you've suffered enough, you say, "God help me, I've suffered enough. Show me the way out." Then you begin a path of searching for a way out. You seek, you search, you do, and you try to undo. You shake and you scream. You sit and stare at a blank wall, you bend yourself into all kinds of *asanas*, you chant, you do workshops, and you read scriptures. You do everything you can to find a way out, out of this mind that is the source of the suffering. If you're lucky, like I was, you run into somebody like Papaji, who says, "Stop, stop it all." The very doing is what's keeping the doer alive. And this doer is the very cause of your suffering. Stop. The seeking postpones the finding; the seeker inhibits the discovery of freedom. Stop. If you are ripe, if you've suffered enough, if you're ready to finish, you listen. You stop seeking, and you become a finder. You trust the words when you hear, "Stop! Be still." The momentum that has been searching for a way out of suffering still continues for a while on its own, but you don't have to participate in it. You'll see the tendency still going, but you know in your heart of hearts that it's finished. The jig is up. You're ready to expose the one who's postponing. You're ready to say, "Enough, I'm finished." You're ready to say to your own Self, "Finish me, whatever it takes, finish me." This is what we come to satsang for: to be finished.

I've been traveling around, offering Prasad's finishing school. It's an opportunity for anyone who still identifies with anything to drop it and be finished, no matter what it is: your search, your doubt, your realization, your ecstasy, your guru. Whatever it is—your religion, your business, your family, everything—renounce it all. This is the message of freedom. If you identify even just a little with anything, then you are still identified with everything. As Papaji used to say, "If you put just one drop of poison in this glass of water, the whole glass of water is poisoned." So you can't just give up the bad stuff, you have to give up everything—and in that giving up, you realize yourself as nothing. Until this happens, every moment of your life is simply a postponement. Your search becomes a postponement, coming to satsang becomes a postponement, reading books becomes a postponement, your goals and relationships become a postponement. Stop postponing! Finish with this search for happiness and realize it here and now, eternally.

We gather together to finish. We don't gather together for any other reason than that. We don't gather together to get anything or to become anyone. In fact, it's the contrary. We gather together in satsang to recognize that we are not someone, which is separate; we are no one, which is Oneness itself. We gather together to reflect each other in this Oneness. It's simple, and yet for so many it's difficult simply to be still, to give up the search, to finish with the doubt, to finish with the excuses and the postponement. If you were on a journey, and you got lost and stopped to ask directions to your destination from somebody you met along the way, and they told you, "You are already here. You've arrived at your destination," what would you do? Would you say, "No, you're wrong. I don't trust you; I don't think this is it. I'm going to keep looking," and get back in your car and keep driving? Some people actually do this. They say, "No, no, it can't be this easy," and then they get back in their car and go search some more. They're attached to the search, the process, the journey. Finish the search. You have arrived; in fact, you never left.

What do you do when you finish? You have been keeping the sufferer alive to motivate you, and now you're finished with it all. Then there's only this moment. There's just this moment, and it reveals itself, like a mystery. You have no idea what's going to happen next. You have no idea where your life will lead and you don't care, because this moment is perfect. The mind rises with its tendencies, and you don't mind it because you've stopped seeking anything else. You've stopped seeking the bliss and the ecstasy. You've stopped spending all your energy working on yourself, trying to improve yourself, trying to get it. So what do you do now? How do you spend your day if you no longer practice? Suddenly, you have a lot of free time! It's like retiring. Anybody who works a full-time job, especially one they don't enjoy fully, looks forward to that day of retirement. So I say, retire now. Take the early retirement plan! Don't postpone, because you never know when your number is up. When you retire, it doesn't mean you sit around and do nothing and watch golf. This is not retirement. Retirement means you stop trying to achieve anything and are available to reap the benefits of just being.

Retire from this rat race, this chasing, this doing. You just have to be willing to do nothing. You have to be willing to stop and to trust that moment of stopping, even though years and years of repressed subconscious beliefs and conditioning may come up. Sometimes it may even be a dark night of the soul: that moment of emptiness when there's nothing to hold on to, nothing you can do, and you're just alone with yourself. Jesus went to the desert for forty days and forty nights and was tempted by the devil. What is the devil but your own mind? God is no-mind; devil must be mind. So you may find yourself in the desert for forty days and forty nights, or however long it takes—the desert means when there is no flowering, no garden, no juice—just dryness, just emptiness. If you're willing to go into the desert inside yourself, renouncing everything, every idea and concept you have of yourself, and do nothing, the devil may rise up to tempt and taunt you. Satan rose up to Jesus and said, "You can have it all, if you will just bow down to me." Isn't this what our minds tell us? "Come on, look at that beautiful girl! You'll be happy if you ask her out. Come on! Look at that beautiful guy. You'll be happy if you make him your husband. Come on! Look at this money. You'll be happy if you get this money. Let's work really hard and make a lot of money, so we can spend it." Is this not the devil tempting you?

B e finished with your search; be finished with your doubt. Be finished with the misidentification with your form as someone or something. Be finished with your concepts and your idea of what freedom looks like, and then be available for Existence to live through you. Whatever shows up, do not be afraid of it. Once you do not doubt, there is nothing to fear. Whatever shows up, you can meet it, even if doubt shows up, because you are free to doubt the doubt. Leave your doubt behind you. Don't take it home with you; it is such a burden. Free your Self from all self-doubt. Let yourselves be finished, and in this finishing, life begins anew. Whoever it is that walked in the door does not have to walk out. Don't carry this "I" with you. Finish with all your doubts and beliefs.

The mind will continue to rise, even in freedom. As long as you have a body, you will have a mind. So those of you who are esoteric seekers, searching for that high state of Nirvana where there will be no mind, where your mind will be a blank slate, where nothing rises, drop that desire! As long as you have a body there will be thoughts related to the body. In fact, the body itself is related to the thought. As long as you have a body, accept that there will be thoughts and desires. Don't make a problem out of them, and don't engage in them. Simply watch them. There will always be thoughts in consciousness. They come and go like streetcars, a streetcar named desire. But you don't have to get on these street-cars, you can just let them pass. You don't have to get on and ride them somewhere, because there's nowhere to go! These thoughts rise and fall like the waves of the ocean. No problem. They are useful, they are creative, they are functional, they create this dream that you are experiencing, but they are not who you are. This is why every religion, every spiritual practice is designed to quiet the mind, whether by chanting mantras or doing yoga, studying scripture or staring at a blank wall. All meditation, all practice is designed to quiet the mind. Now that you are quiet, I will tell you the truth: you, as you believe yourself to be, do not exist.

How do you realize your Self? First, realize who you are not. In India this is referred to as *neti neti:* not this and not that. First of all, you're not these bodies, and you're not these minds that worry about these bodies. You're not these personalities, and you're surely not these lives you're leading. You're not this "I" who believes anything or who believes something. You're not this "me" who needs to express his or her truth, or seek his or her desire, or run from his or her fear. You're not any of this. You're not who you think you are. If you're open to the possibility of letting go of who you believe yourself to be, of not knowing where you're coming from and not knowing where you're going in this moment, if you're open to let go, you can taste the truth of who you are. It only takes a second.

The mind is nothing but an addict. The mind that you believe yourself to be will never be satisfied; it will never have enough knowledge, power, love, joy, peace. As long as you still believe that somehow your dreams will be fulfilled, your goals will be attained, your desires will be satisfied, then you are only one split second away from suffering. When you finally admit that the mind will never have enough and will constantly be searching for more, then you're at the threshold of recognizing your own true Self. But remember, your mind is an addict, not you, so don't mind your mind, no matter what rises. This is how people kick addictions. You have an urge for a cigarette, but you've made it clear that you're not going to smoke. You'll do everything else but! You'll chew gum, wear a patch, suck on a pencil, but you won't light up. That's how you finally quit. You say, "I won't light up, no matter what," and you don't. Each day it becomes a little easier. It's the same thing with dropping the mind.

Desires come; desires go. If they play themselves out, let them play themselves out. If they do not, don't mind that either. Simply don't mind your mind. This is how you can live in sustainable freedom. This is the key. The first step is to detach from your thoughts and to recognize that you aren't your mind. Each time the mind rises, you watch, and simply allow it to return to Emptiness. Don't identify with it. Don't engage in it. Don't resist it. Don't try to control it. Don't do anything! Be still, no matter what happens. And in that stillness, everything that your mind was looking for is available. Everything that your mind was hoping you would feel if you got those particular desires fulfilled, you're feeling already. You are That! So why go the long way down the yellow brick road, when you are already there.

Where are you still identified? Where do you still believe that the story you're playing is real? When you believe it, when you're engaged in it—this is what takes you out of silence, the silent witnessing. Where do you take yourself too seriously in your life? What about your life is so important that it disturbs your peace? True freedom is recognizing that your health, wealth, and relationships come and go, so don't base your happiness on them. Freedom is allowing yourself not to know. So, don't know! Don't know who you are, don't know what's important, don't know where you are going, and certainly don't know where you have come from.

Simply do not know who you are and the truth of who you are reveals itself. Let go of that thought that tells you who you think you are—it limits you. It shows up in desire; it shows up in reaction; it shows up in fear, and it limits you. It only takes one look to recognize your own Self, but only those who are ripe recognize it. What is this ripeness? It's an availability to truth. It's a willingness to let go of the mind. It's a willingness to admit that everything you have believed up until this moment is a lie. Nothing is true. Truth is who you are! It's not a concept. It's not something to be attained, and it's not something you can lose. This ripeness is usually the result of suffering. When the someone who is identified has suffered enough, then he is willing to drop his identity, which is the source of his suffering.

Self realization is not a path; it's not a technique; it's not a process; it's the direct realization of your true nature by seeing who you are not, by recognizing that whoever you identify yourself as being in this moment is a lie. By breaking free from your misidentification with your past, with your story, and dropping the idea that you have come from anywhere or are going anywhere, you become still and available to this moment. In this stillness, the truth reveals itself to itself. This is not some esoteric religion or some particular technique that only can be achieved by some; this is available to everyone because there is only one of us. There is only One and it is your own Self. When you're ready to finish with your playthings, your neuroses, your worries, your fears, your doubts and your desires—you will be available to realize this truth.

Once you realize Self, you go about your business. You live your life, you work your jobs, you have your babies, and you enjoy the drama of your life. Nothing has to change. Sometimes, the old habits fall away because you don't have to be afraid anymore. You don't have to desire to be something other than what you are in this moment. Energy is freed up that you once used to avoid, to control, to resist, to manipulate. These defenses disappear in surrender. You now have a lot of free energy, a lot of love to share, to serve, to create. This is what is available in freedom, not to look for something more, not to work on ourselves, but simply to celebrate the truth. Those of you who haven't tasted it yet, make yourselves available. For one moment, don't know who you are! Don't have any plans; have no history; just be this moment. Be available in this moment and watch what happens.

There is nothing you need to do. Just open your heart to your own Self. See your mind and how it constantly separates you from this love that you are, how it constantly wants to be something or somebody you're not, how it constantly judges the moment as imperfect. Just drop this mind! Whenever it rises, pay no attention to it. Surrender to the love that you are. And if life doesn't show up the way you like it, if you find yourself getting distracted, chasing some idle thought or desire, then come back to the love that you are in this Emptiness. The mind gets distracted by what it views as important, whatever it is, and it's different for everyone. What you view as important engages your consciousness. That's why some of your most cherished ideals are dashed in satsang. Some of the most crystallized concepts that you're holding onto so desperately are being challenged here in satsang—and this is a good thing, like spring cleaning. You're going through your attic and you're throwing out what's there, and you think, "Oh no, I can't throw these out! These are my cherished memories." Then your house burns down, and if you're attached to those items, there's tremendous suffering—but if you can let go of those identifications, there's a sense of relief.

Don't be afraid to burn up. Bring your stuff to satsang, and we will burn it. Take all of the stuff that you are carrying in your attic, make a bonfire right here, and burn it up until there is nothing left! Take your most sacred beliefs and set them on fire. For some of you, the fire burns bright and it glows, and the light is almost blinding. It is so beautiful! For others, if you are attached, the fire is horrific and you wonder, "Why is my life falling apart, now that I am coming to satsang?" The fire burns bright and whatever needs to fall away, falls away; whatever needs to be illuminated is illuminated; and whatever needs to be melted is melted. How long the fire has to burn depends on how much stuff you still have in your attic. So have a yard sale first, give everything away! Don't hang on to it. Be willing to let it all go.

There was a Zen master who came home and found his house on fire. The neighbors were all pouring buckets of water on it, and they had taken what furniture they could save and removed it before the fire got too bad. When the master arrived, he started to take his furniture and throw it back into the house to let it burn. The neighbors were aghast! Then, suddenly, it started raining, and the rain was putting out the fire, so the master picked up the buckets of water and began throwing water on the fire until it was extinguished. Afterwards, when the neighbors asked him about his strange behavior, he replied, "When I came home Existence was burning my house, so I helped it. And then when Existence began putting it out, I also helped it." So Existence is here to burn you, consume you in the flames of freedom. Let this burning desire for freedom finish you! This is all it takes in satsang, I promise you. It only takes a burning desire for freedom. Now, that doesn't mean it'll be pleasant when your ego is consumed by the flames of truth. That doesn't mean it will feel good to the ego. It means freedom can be realized in this moment, and truth can burn brightly in your heart.

There has to be a burning desire for freedom, almost obsessive—meaning, there's no place else, there's nothing else you'd rather be doing than being in satsang, than sitting in truth. Nothing else does it for you. Like any burning desire, it consumes you and all that remains is Emptiness. When it's a burning desire for anything else, when any other desire consumes you, it also leaves you with a kind of emptiness, but because it was a desire for something other than Emptiness, it feels awful. You desire fame; you desire money; you desire relationship; and it doesn't come. It's an obsessive desire. You've all been there; you've done it; you've obsessed, trying to get something. Then it didn't come, and you felt completely empty. Or maybe it came and went: you found the lover you'd been seeking for lifetimes; then she disappeared, and you were left feeling empty. Because Emptiness was not your desire, you felt miserable. You see? If you desire Emptiness, if that is your last desire, then that desire will consume all other desires. When you allow your desires to be burned up, suffering burns up with it.

The fire of truth is burning bright: let it consume you. Let it finish whatever doubts you have that you are not already free. Let it burn away whatever desires you have for something else in order to be happy. Let it finish any postponements, any conditions you have, any judgments, and any fears you have. Let it finish. Let the fire of satsang finish you, until all that remains are ashes—and from these ashes, the truth of who you are rises. Brand new, unsmelled, untasted, unknown, and it happens every moment in freedom. It's a continual burning of who you have believed yourself to be, and then the phoenix rises from the ashes and you discover who you are right now. What a joy!

Come close to the fire so you can burn. The closer you get the hotter it gets. All of your concepts, all of your ideas, all of your comforts and your comfort zone itself begin to be challenged when you get this close to the fire. It's as if you've been living inside a wax figure, a statue that you've believed yourself to be. The closer you get to the fire, this wax begins to melt and old attachments begin to dissolve. If you try to grab them as they're melting, you get burned. This is what happens with hot wax! But if you just let them melt away, what remains is who you are. This is how the grace of satsang serves you. Sometimes, when you first come it feels good, because that wax was stiff for ages. It feels good, a little mobility. Then the fire continues to burn in places where you're not sure you want so much mobility. You're not sure you want to move out of your comfort zone, your dreams and wishes of what you believe to be a good life. In satsang, all of these conditions are challenged in the face of unconditional freedom. Unconditional freedom means not a drop of wax, no more identification with the wax figure, just the pure, fluid formlessness that remains when the wax is melted.

When it gets too hot, sometimes you find yourself running away. This is all part of the melting; trust even that. The moth dances with the light for a while, gets closer, moves away. It hovers around it, feels the heat, and then is drawn to the light. Eventually, it goes straight for the center, and the moth is no more. All that remains is the light. Let it burn; don't be afraid. Whatever burns away is just the wax; it's necessary to drop this misidentification with story, with form, so that you can be free. Underneath this wax you're already free! Before the story, after the story, you are always free. But when the story rises, you're dunking yourself in the vat of hot wax, and before you know it, you're solidified again, encrusted with your beliefs and your ideas.

Let the grace of satsang burn it all away by itself. Burn away whatever it is you think is holding you back from living in the totality of your being-ness. This is your opportunity to end all suffering. The closer you get to the fire, the more accelerated it is. If you pull away, you harden again, and you wonder, "What happened? Why am I suffering again? What happened to my peace; what happened to my bliss? I feel all crusty again; I don't feel free." It's because you pulled away from the fire of your own Self, burning that which is unnecessary, that which is untrue. Let yourself burn. Let yourself be finished with this sufferer—then there is no more suffering, there is just life unfolding. Whatever is in the way, expose it, and burn it up. Whatever cherished belief system you hold about yourself, burn it up. This is what's happening here in satsang. You only have to come and be available, and it happens by itself. This availability means not running away when the heat gets too hot. It means welcoming the issues when they come up, so that you can be finished with them. It means meeting your fears, not running from them. It means watching your desires, not chasing after them. It means being willing to let go of your attachments and accept your aversions. Let yourself burn up. Let the leftover attachments, desires, and fears that are taking you out of silence burn up and trust what remains.

Just have the commitment. Say, "This truth is all I want," and all of your other desires get burned up by that one desire for truth and freedom. No matter what is given to you and no matter what is taken away from you, it doesn't touch you, because you are this constant. The freedom that you are doesn't change; it's always here. This is what you rely on. It's always here. Nothing can touch you—you're free! It really is easy to live in freedom. It takes a lot more effort to chase your desires, to try to make your life work. It takes a lot more effort to stay in this illusion of bondage, this illusion of trying to attain. Stop trying to attain anything. Keep still and watch. Watch your life work and not work, be happy, be sad, whatever. Get out of your own way. Let it happen. It takes a lot less effort to live this way! Stop being a busy body, and be nobody.

D on't let yourself get distracted. Don't let yourself get distracted by bliss. Bliss ain't it! It's just a symptom, and symptoms come and go. Freedom does not come and go. Find out the constant that is always present—no matter whether you like or dislike, whether you're with a lover or alone, whether you're broke or wealthy. Find out what the constant is that doesn't change and marry that. Don't marry some fleeting emotion or some fleeting epiphany or some temporary high. Then you'll be so busy chasing, you'll wonder what happened! Devote yourself to your commitment to truth, and you'll see that you're already awakened; it's just a delusion that you're asleep. You don't actually do anything to wake up. Whatever you try to do to wake up makes the idea that you're not awake more real.

Use whatever shows up as a device to finish what stands in the way, and finish the "I." Be humble enough to let yourself get slapped around if it's needed, or let yourself be kissed if it's needed, because freedom is more important than your pride. Freedom is more important than the way you appear to your colleagues, to your community. Freedom is more important than the attainment of anything, for freedom is the attainment of nothing. The constant vigilance to nothing is the only way to remain empty. Give up everything, and anything that rises—let it rise and let it fall. It is happening already. Be quiet. Let your life fall apart if it falls apart. Let your life blossom if it's blossoming. To everything there's a season.

Make nothing more important than God, my love. Make God your top desire, more than the health of your body, more than your children, and more than your lover. Trust God and God will provide for all of those and more. Now when I say, "Trust God," make no mistake, I'm not speaking of somebody outside of you. I'm speaking of your very own Self, who you are, your very nature. I am telling your mind to keep quiet and trust. This is all. When you keep quiet and trust, the God that you are takes over. It just takes over. It has already taken over, but you realize it and you stop resisting. You stop the delusion that you are controlling anything. You wake up from this dream that you have any choice in your life. You see that this mind is deluded to think that it has any free will. What the mind calls free will is nothing but choosing between maybe two or three possibilities: fight, flight, or get a lawyer! This is not free will! It's just doing the same old, same old over and over, perhaps with different colors and different costumes, lifetime after lifetime.

Make the desire to serve God, to live as God, to share God, and to be God your number one priority. Make your commitment to live in freedom, to speak freedom, to live as truth, to express truth—make it all there is. As Jesus said, "Seek ye first the kingdom of heaven, and all the rest will follow." Stop looking for satisfaction outside of yourself; stop trying to figure it out. Stop doubting; stop defending, and just be. Be free. Be love, it's your nature; it's who you are. Tell the mind to keep quiet. Don't buy into it; don't believe it, and see the perfection of the moment. No matter what you think, it is perfect. Trust the perfection no matter what. This is what it takes: faith, surrender, and the commitment to truth and freedom.

Freedom is unattainable when you are busy chasing something else. It may seem that, for a second, you have it, when you attain whatever it is: success in your job, success in your relationship. For that second, when your desires have been fulfilled, you feel it, but then what happens? The desire rises for something else. The fear of losing what you've got rises to disturb your peace, and you're off and running again. Freedom is desirelessness. Don't engage! Trust Existence. It will give you exactly what you need, whether or not it's what you want. Who cares? Only mind. See the perfection of this moment, for you are That.

Know that it's all perfect. When this happens, when you let yourself realize this truth, then the rest of your life takes on a flavor of pure acceptance, pure grace, pure love, and a complete understanding of how perfect your life already is. Everything that has happened, is happening, and will happen is a perfect manifestation of who you are. How can it be otherwise? When you recognize this, you'll stop trying to change yourself, stop trying to improve yourself, stop trying to work on yourself—and you'll put the therapists and the religions out of business! Along with all the self-help books, the health clubs, and the diet programs, you'll put them out of business when you get that you are perfect just the way you are. This is the greatest diet that there is: Prasad's miracle-diet! This is when you fast from your mind! You say, "No more 'I' this week; I take a break from 'I.' I'm just available to the pure, free love." Free love has no calories. It's so nourishing, and it is the Source of who you are.

You are perfect just the way you are. You are perfection itself. This is why you admire your guru so much, because she's perfect. This is why you admire the saints and the masters, because they're perfect. "Oh, Lord Buddha, you are perfect." Of course you see the Buddha as perfect because the Buddha sees himself as perfect! But he also sees you as perfect, because he doesn't see anybody as separate. Allow the Buddha that you are to be present here and now. Recognize yourself as the Messiah, and save your own ass! Be the master and stop thinking it's outside of you. You are the master; I can't convince you of it, but I can invite you to drop your judging mind. When you do, you will see what I see—because there is only One of us. You are perfection itself.

Do you get how perfect you are? Not for any reason, but because you are. Everything is evolving perfectly. Everything is expressing itself in perfection—and your egos, they are perfect too. Accept them; accept your egos. As I always say, "Love your egos; love them to death." Accept them: stop trying to change them, stop trying to improve them, stop trying to get them to become enlightened. Your ego will never get enlightened. In truth there's nothing you can do to improve yourself. You can change yourself, surely, but you can't improve yourself. Whatever you are is already perfect. Get that, and then play! Abide as the creator and enjoy your creation. Let it be whatever it is, stop imposing something on it, and have fun with whatever is. It will change, because everything changes, and then you will get to play with something else. If you resist it, if you are identified with it—it is going to get stale, it is going to get old, it is going to get rotten. Just accept the whole dance, but don't get caught up in your lives. Don't be so involved in them.

What is there to do once you've realized your perfection? What do you do once you've stopped seeking? What do you do once you've realized Self? You do nothing! It's all done for you. You do absolutely nothing. There is nobody left to identify with any of it, and you sit and you stand and you walk and you lie down, and truth is in every moment. There's nobody left to do anything. There's nobody left to take responsibility for anything. There's nobody left to take credit for anything—and there's nobody left to take the blame for anything either! You are out of your own way, and Existence pulses through you. Your whole life is the dance of Existence. Every motion, every lifting of the hand is done by Existence; every word that falls from your lips is Existence's. You cannot take responsibility for anything: if you write books, you can't put your name on them; if you make dinner, you can't even say I made dinner. You can't take responsibility for anything you do, because it is Existence's doing. In truth, you are Existence. I don't mean this "I" who thinks he is doing, but this vastness that is your true nature. Once you realize your Self as Existence, once you drop this false "I," you see that everything you do is an expression of Existence.

If you don't know who you are, then you're nobody. If you're nobody, then Truth is. The minute you think you're somebody—somebody who is enlightened; somebody who isn't enlightened; somebody who's trying to get enlightened; somebody who's a disciple; somebody who's a guru; somebody who's a husband; somebody who's a wife, a son, a daughter; white, black, Catholic, Hindu, whatever— the minute you think you're somebody, you're living a lie, and that lie becomes your bondage. In freedom you don't know who you are. Ever! This is Self-Realization. Not knowing who you are is realizing Self. Thinking you know who you are is just a mind trip. When you're nobody, you can be anybody. So who are you when there's no "I"? It can't be spoken. It can't be told. It can only be pointed to.

Who are you when there's no "I"? This is the only question. In order to find out the answer to that question, you have to look at the "I." You have to look when it rises and see what keeps it identified, what keeps it believing in itself as real. What are the attachments, the desires? What are the fears that motivate this "I" to perpetuate itself? Look directly at the "I" and see through its ridiculous scheme to make itself real. Once you see through it, then there's full permission for this "I" to rise and fall. In each moment the "I" re-creates itself, adapting with the deftness of a magician, changing costumes moment by moment, playing whatever role it wants to play—but if it's seen clearly by you as a role, as not real, there's no identification. When there's no identification, there's freedom, pure freedom, and it doesn't matter what happens in the circumstances of your life, or the emotional reactions to those circumstances. It doesn't matter because you've seen through the "I." You've exposed it as a concept, as a belief, as merely a thought, "Everything I've believed myself to be up until this moment, every problem, every celebration, everyone I've loved, every struggle, every victory—it's all merely a concept, an idea." This is the greatest victory of all, when you're silent, when you see through your "I."

Everything that rises in your consciousness is concept. Freedom is recognizing this and not touching anything. Fear rises, attachment to comfort rises, the pursuit of other than what is rises; they're just concepts. You don't put any attention or energy on what is concept; you keep quiet. No matter how significant you think it is, just be still. In the stillness, revelation happens by itself in a sustainable way, because it's not a concept. You haven't bought what somebody has told you. You haven't taken it on from outside of you. It's recognized as your own truth, and this sets you free. You're never held prisoner again by your mind. You're never held hostage by your emotions. You're free!

You can relax. You can just be. You don't have to be somebody; you don't have to be right. You don't have to help anybody; you don't have to save the world, you don't have to write your masterpiece—you don't have to do anything! You can just forget about it, and when you do, the silence is available. The silence is God-Consciousness. Just keep quiet. This is the secret for freedom: don't mind your mind. Never mind your mind when it is telling you, "You are free," and never mind your mind when it's telling you, "You are in bondage." Never mind your mind when it tells you, "This is it!" Never mind your mind when it tells you, "This is not it." Just keep quiet and the perfection of this moment presents itself. You see that you are in heaven right now and it's perfect. Don't mind your mind: it's bullshit. It's all B.S. — belief systems. The ego is full of B.S. The Self is full of grace. When you admit that you are full of it, grace is what is left, this silent, vast grace. And the beauty is, even the bullshit rises from this grace, so it's perfect too. It's all divine. It's all grace. It's only your mind that tells you otherwise.

The "I" forgets that it's grace, forgets that it's love, forgets that it's God. It looks outside in search of grace, in search of love, or in search of God, and it will never find it because it is It. You are It! The "I" is just the veil that obscures this realization of grace. Pierce this veil. Look at this "I" and be finished with it—finally! Don't be afraid to look at the "I." Don't be afraid to admit where you're selfish, where you're afraid, where you're still caught in desire; to admit where you're attached. You must look at the "I" to be finished with the "I." When it rises, and you find your "I" dangling over a cliff, and the "I" is scared—this is beautiful because you can see it. Then it drops by itself! Don't be afraid to look at the "I." This is how you free yourself from the identification with it.

In freedom, "I" rises: if you are watching it, no problem; if you are not, if you are identified with it, it will appear as if you are no longer free. Look at your "I." It's no coincidence that the word *identification* begins with "I," the word *issues* begins with the letter "I," the word *insecurity* begins with the letter "I." Look at your identifications, your issues, and your insecurities. If you're fearless about freedom, if you're committed to the realization of the grace that you are, then you can simply say, "Bring it on. Bring it on; give it to me! Bring on my issues, bring on my identification, bring on my insecurities, so that I can see them and be finished with them once and for all!" If you see the "I," it falls away. This is how we live in freedom. Don't be afraid to look at the "I." If you look at the "I," then you are the Awareness looking.

Notice your I-thought when it rises. "There's my old story; it's not who I am," and it falls away. "There's my old issue, once again, coming to tickle my karmic funny bone." Don't be afraid of it. Don't try to pretend that you don't have issues; don't try to deny identification when it's there. Look at the "I," admit that the "I" is rising, and it will fall. If you are hiding, then you are identified with the "I" who's afraid, who doesn't see itself as perfect, who doesn't know that it is grace. Don't be afraid to look at the "I"; don't be afraid to acknowledge that your story is rising. Admit it and drop it. This is how you can abide in freedom. If you see the "I," the "I" dissolves—because there's someone aware, someone awake who does not believe in it. If you are hiding, the "I" bites you, controls you, and dominates your life. Sometimes this "I" pretends to be spiritual: it learns all the right words, develops itself to fit in so that it can stick around. See through it; see through this veil called "I" to the Source of who you are before it rises, before it's believed in. You can abide quietly; you can abide in silence. No matter what story rises and falls, it doesn't touch you.

Don't be afraid to face your issues; don't be afraid to let emotions rise; don't be afraid to let the desires come and go. Be aware and let them be finished. Don't run from them, don't deny them, and don't hide from them. See if there's any more "I" that's hiding, any more "I" that's attached, any more "I" that's denying, and expose it. Look at it directly. Have the courage, the faith, and the love to look at your ego honestly, authentically, so that it can fall away and you can keep quiet. Pierce this veil called "I" and see the truth of who you are in this instant. Whatever identification, whatever issue, whatever insecurity may arise, don't be afraid to look at it. Be finished with it, so that you can keep still and abide in grace, abide in love, abide as the master that you are. The "I" never touches the master. Be honest with yourselves. Expose this "I" if it's still there. If it's not, it will be seen clearly that you are I-less, that you are free, and then there's only confirmation. There's only reflection of freedom and truth. But if there's still an "I" there, if there's still a little doubt that you are grace, it can be exposed and dropped in satsang. Even just a little bit of doubt can contaminate the abidance in the truth of who you are. So expose this doubt, expose this "I." Don't be afraid to look at the ego. When you look at it, you free yourself.

People have spent years and years trying to get the ego to cooperate. They do all kinds of practices, and it just makes the ego that much more real. Oh, good ego! The ego says, "Aren't I good? See, I can stand on my head. I do all kinds of yoga positions. See, aren't I good? I'm serving the world; I'm Mother Teresa. Wow, aren't I good?" This is all ego. Freedom is realizing you are not your ego. That's all. Stop trying to make your minds go away and just let them be. So what if your mind rises. Who cares? It rises in your dreams. Do you try to control your dreams? Do you try to have good dreams? Does it work? You can't control your dreams; you surrender in your dream life. Why can't you in this life? Because you think it's real.

Who needs to fight your mind? You don't have to confront your mind—it will disappear; it is just a dream. If you think your mind is real, then you think you have to work with it, deal with it, process or express it, transcend it. That's making it more real! All you have to do is see through it; look at the thought and see that it's a thought. This is what all your years of meditation have prepared you for. You are not in denial when you say a thought is not true, because the fact is, it's not true. Are you in denial when you tell your imaginary friend to disappear? Are you in denial when you stop believing your mind? How can you deny something that's not there? You can't fight a phantom; you'll end up falling flat on your face.

on't be afraid of your egos. Don't be afraid of your minds. Let them come and go. Let them play themselves out while you remain vigilant as the watcher, as the pure Awareness that you are. Some days it's pure stillness; nothing's happening. Some days it's turbulence, and you just can't understand. "Yesterday, I was feeling so peaceful, and today I'm a wreck!" You just inquire, "Who's a wreck? It's just a wrecking thought, a wrecking ball coming through my life to shake things up." Your Consciousness is stuck on some thought or is abiding in some thought called, "me," whoever you believe yourself to be. Then your life progresses from this. You see your patterns; you go to therapy to work on them, read the books, or meditate—it's the theme of your life. See it clearly: there's my story. Then it drops, and in that Emptiness, the whole dream takes on a different flavor. The whole dream becomes heaven, no longer hell, no longer purgatory. No longer struggling, just heaven, because you've let go of any concepts that take you out of heaven. You've accepted yourself totally in this moment, thoughts and all.

You don't have to be afraid of your mind any longer. You don't have to be afraid of your story, no matter how painful it once was or appeared to be. This is just a concept. Keep still, be quiet, and know nothing. Know absolutely nothing and you're the Buddha. Know something and you're just another mind, filled with concepts and ideas that come and go. We sit in satsang together not to get anything, but to drop everything. Just drop whatever you came with, whatever it was. Even if it's something you realized in satsang, drop it. It's now a story. Don't spend energy trying to make your mind be quiet, and don't be afraid when your mind rises. Just be aware and see that it's mind. Who cares? It's going to fall as quickly as it rose. "Maybe I can actually enjoy it for a couple of minutes. I'm having one of those days; I'm just feeling lonely today. Who's feeling lonely? I am." Then you take out a little puppet and you do "the lonely puppet." Your egos are puppets, nothing more. "I'm feeling hopeless, absolutely hopeless; it's futile," says the hopeless puppet. It's no big deal! Don't make a big deal out of your mind. You have to be willing to drop your stories. Just drop them.

Love your ego…love your ego to death. It doesn't mean the ego gets her own way; it doesn't mean the ego has to run the show. It doesn't even mean the ego gets what he wants. But it means, in your abidance in truth as the Source of who you are, you have tremendous compassion and tolerance for your ego. You see the ego. You see the judgments of your mind, you see the fear of your I-thought, and there's just compassion for it because you know it's not real. You love it; you just love it. You don't try to change it, and you don't judge it. If you judge it, it constricts and resists. It judges you and keeps you stuck. In freedom, there's no judgment necessary. Everything is seen as perfect. When you are non-identified with this ego, everything is grace, everything is flowing. Not because it fits your ego's picture of what a flow is, but because you're in tune with what is, instead of what you want or what you're afraid of.

Ego grasps, ego resists, ego is all about control, but you can't control the ego. If you try to control it, it just fusses more. Look for yourselves, with all of your disciplines and all of your routines and all of your goals. The more you try to control ego the more it resists. So accept it; accept who you are in this lifetime, in this dream. Accept your role; accept your character. When you accept your ego, the ego can be worked with. When you don't deny it, when you don't pretend it's not there, when you admit and accept and love it, then it dies by itself. You don't have to kill your ego. You just have to realize it's already dead! It's already dead, but it's keeping itself alive because you've been paying attention to it. You've been resisting it, judging it, trying to control it. Just realize it is already dead, and this dead ego needs to go. It needs to go because it's garbage! Take it out to the curb and let the trash man take it. Bury the past with all that's dead, and don't touch the future. Just be here now, open and available to be surprised by the aliveness of this moment.

Don't engage; don't cling to the known because then you're dead, and you're riding the known in a hearse right to the graveyard! It will always take you to that which is already dead. The known is dead; the unknown is aliveness. The known is ego. Ego is afraid of the unknown; ego is afraid of aliveness. Ego is dead. If you know who you are, you're dead! Find out who you are by letting go of who you know you are. It's this simple! Don't know who you are in this moment. Be unknown, be unmanifest and watch the moment reveal itself. When Jesus was gathering his disciples, two brothers wanted to go back to their father's funeral, and Jesus said, "Don't worry about it. Let the dead bury the dead. There's plenty of dead in your village. Come, and I'll show you eternal life."

Don't worry about that which is already past. Don't mind it; it's gone. Just be here now in the aliveness of this unknown moment. That's all it takes to abide in freedom. And if somebody arises—somebody familiar from your past, some whiney, complaining victim, some guy who's totally attached to his misery—then you inquire, "Who cares? Who's attached? I am. Well who does this 'I' think he is anyway?" Then the "I" falls away, right back from where it rose, right back into silence. "Who am I?" There's no answer to this question; it's not known, it's only unknown. This question, "Who am I?" takes you right back into the unknown instantly.

This moment is brand new. This moment is reborn; you're born again. This is what baptism is, but it's a baptism of fire in each moment. This is what it is to live awake. You have no continuity. It's total in this moment. And if this moment appears to have something to do with the next moment, it's just a coincidence. It's just your mind connecting the dots. Each moment is a dot; don't connect them. You don't have to understand it; you don't have to figure it out; you don't have to make sense of it. The dot is fine on its own. When you're awake, you can just get into the dot. It's so multi-leveled, so multifaceted—this dot, this moment—and yet you're already looking for the next dot. You're eating the appetizer and wondering what the main course will be, and when the main course comes, you are all ready for dessert. This moment is so deep, so rich, so full—it's brand new. Die to the past and recognize That which you are. Be willing to start over each moment. This is how it is in freedom, no continuity. The now is just a dot, just a moment. Only the mind connects the dots and carries a story into the next moment.

When you realize you're nobody, there's no history, no herstory, nothing. Nothing to bog you down, nothing in your way, there's just this pure, pristine moment, which is infinite possibility. You start fresh. This is what baptism is. You are all baptized in this moment. It means you are fresh, new, free of original sin. For what is original sin, but the mind? The mind thinks. It started way back when Adam gave Eve the apple from the tree of knowledge of good and evil. I am rewriting the story: Adam gave it to Eve, Adam disguised as a serpent. Then they left paradise. They ate from the tree of knowledge of good and evil and then they left paradise. If you want to return to paradise, give up this knowledge. Be empty. Be innocent. Be available. Then you find you're in paradise. You've always been in paradise! It was your own mind disguised as the serpent that took you out of paradise, "Come on! Taste it! Mmm, delicious! It's called knowledge." You see? Knowledge! The devil tempts you with the knowledge of right and wrong. You've now tasted duality and then you fall out of paradise.

When we were babies, we were pure God living in paradise, which is no mind. You only have to look into a baby's eyes to see this: pure God. Then the personality developed; defense, fear, abandonment, control, and pleasing Mommy and Daddy. Return to paradise, my loves! Cast the devil out, and you are in paradise. Papaji says it like this: "Don't think." I'm using biblical terms: cast the devil out! Don't think—and you are in paradise, where you have always been. It's just that you went through a dream in which you ate from the tree of knowledge and got cast out, and were ashamed. Ashamed! How many people have an unworthiness story? Is everybody not Adam and Eve? You see, Adam and Eve didn't really happen. Everybody who's studied Charles Darwin knows that, but Adam and Eve are happening now! You are Adam and you are Eve. And every time you eat from the tree of knowledge of good and evil, you cast yourself out of paradise. You let the devil take you from pure Consciousness into some limited idea of who you are. It happens over and over. So, ask yourself, "What is my story that takes me out of paradise?" Renounce it to find yourself back in paradise.

There is no lasting value to anything that you think or anything that comes and goes, be it your most sacred relationship or your most painful fear, so step outside of duality. If you take credit for your life, you have to take the blame. If you believe the good reviews, and the approval, you have to believe the bad reviews and the disapproval. Drop it all. See that this need for approval is just the other side of the fear of disapproval. The pursuit of beauty is the opposite of the aversion to ugliness. Seeking peace is running from conflict. There's no freedom; it's just rebelling against your own point of view! Your mind is in conflict with itself, and you call this your spiritual path! Religions are filled with this. There's no freedom; it's just one opposing thought conflicting with another thought. Freedom is thoughtless, beginning-less, and endless. If it begins, it will end. If you achieve it, you will lose it. Realize what is already here; realize what is already present. You don't have to do anything to achieve it. It's right here, right now, always, and it's all you can depend on.

Whatever happens in the domain of duality, don't mind it. One moment you feel ugly, the next moment, beautiful. One moment you love your beloved; the next moment you hate her. One moment you feel lost and cloudy; the next moment you feel found in clarity. All of it is irrelevant. All that is relevant is the truth of who you are. That does not change. That does not exist within the domain of duality. If it comes, it goes. This is the nature of duality: night and day, birth and death, giving and receiving, inhaling and exhaling. How do we live in the Oneness of freedom within this domain of duality? How can we embrace the dark as well as the light? How can we receive while giving, and give while receiving? How can we be still while moving, silent while speaking, and at peace while the whole world around us is collapsing? The secret is by saying "yes" to what comes and saying "yes" to what goes. Saying "yes" to the pleasure and saying "yes" to the pain. Saying "yes" to what you have and saying "yes" to what you have not. Saying "yes" to the positive, and to the negative as well, creates a balance between these polar opposites. You hang out between the two in the witness, just watching. It's like a pyramid, negative and positive at the base and you at the top, watching. You only have to look on the back of a dollar bill to see this metaphor, with its single eye watching from above.

Advaita is the simple truth that there's only One. There are no two. Mind is fragmented; mind creates two. First there is I, then there is you. First there is observer, then there is observed, and there is always separation in these two. Whenever there's an other, there's separation. Yoga means union, the ultimate finishing. The completion of all yoga is union, oneness. The only difference between advaita and other paths of yoga is that it is clearly seen that you are already in union. The whole idea of having to attain it, or do some practice to achieve it, is completely an illusion. It's a concept, and this very concept is what can keep you in separation. This is why my Master, Papaji, would tell us to do nothing. He would tell us to drop our practice and to keep still. In this stillness, the truth—that we are already in union, we are already One—becomes obvious. This truth, this absolute truth that there is no other, that there's only one, becomes so present in this stillness. When there's no longer some body trying to achieve some thing, then it is clearly seen that we are already that which we seek. There are many paths, and ultimately, all paths prepare you for this moment, this moment when you can recognize: I am already here. I am already One. There is only One, and I am That. Any appearance of two is just the projection of my mind. It's just a dream. It's just a concept rising in Awareness.

You are the creator of your world, and you are also your creation. You are the observer, but you are also the observed. You are the subject, and in a way, you are also the object. When the subject and the object become one, when the observer and the observed become one, when the creator and the creation are seen as one—then nothing remains. The two I's become one. This one is not some one; this one is no one. There's no observer, just pure observation. There's no creator, just pure creativity, pure witnessing, pure Awareness. There are many paths to this moment, yet eventually you find yourself here, so why not start here? Why postpone? Start here and recognize that I am the creator and the creation. I am form, and I am the formlessness in which this form rises. And if I am the formlessness, then I am all forms; all forms rise within me. Just like when you're dreaming at night, your whole world rises inside of your Consciousness as a part of your Consciousness, a whole world with a whole cast of characters. Who created these characters? Who creates the world when you're dreaming at night? You do. It's the same in this waking world. This is your dream, welcome to it.

When you go to sleep at night, a whole world is created within you, a whole dream world with dream characters. Whole universes rise and fall within your consciousness when you're asleep and dreaming. Such beautiful stories you create: sometimes fun, sometimes scary, sometimes sexy. Is there ever any doubt that you create these stories? When you wake up, you realize, "I never left; I've been here all along." You never doubt that it all happened inside of you. You know it was a dream—but while you're having the dream, it doesn't appear this way. It appears that you are in a body, in a world, traveling around, doing your thing with no doubt that the dream is real. Wake up and realize that everything you perceive is happening within you! This is the dream! It doesn't make the experience any less; it just puts it in perspective. The world is in you; there is no other. There is only the projection of your own Self that appears to be outside of you. Abide in the source of this projection. Then there's no separation, there's only Oneness, and you can enjoy the dance of apparent separation. It doesn't matter what happens in that dance. You can be fighting or you can be making love. It doesn't matter when you know that you're One.

Each night you don't continue the saga of your dreams. No, it's a whole new dream; each night it's fresh. It rises from Emptiness—even though it's your mind, it's mind rising from Emptiness. This life, this dream has the same possibility. The form only appears to be the same to your mind, but this moment is fresh and new. The air you're breathing is fresh and new, the cells in your body are fresh and new. Be empty, be this newness, be this infinite possibility and then any miracle can happen! When you see the old thought, the old memory, the old mind rising, ignore it. Don't mind it; don't limit your experience by it. Wake up from this dream and enjoy it—celebrate it! This is just another dream. You're playing out your life in these dreams; you're playing out your unconscious impulse to explore what it is to be.

D on't listen with your minds. Be still. Let go of all that is known in this moment. Surrender to the unknown. If your eyes are closed, open them. If your eyes are open, close them and see there is no difference. Inner and outer, it is the same. It is all dream. Look deeply at the Source. In the stillness of this present moment, let your past and future disappear and be stranded in this moment. No place to go. This is realizing the perfection that you are. If this moment were the last moment of your existence in this body, if this breath were to be your last breath, could you say that it is perfect? Could you accept this moment as the final culmination of your life in this body? Live like this, my love.

When you are analyzing your dreams with your therapist, how many times do you say, "It should have been different"? Never, you just describe the dream. You don't say, "I wish it was a blue Volkswagen instead of a purple one." You don't say, "I wish I had taken the bus instead of flying." You don't say, "I wish there were three of me instead of only one." You just let the dream be; you report the dream. You're not invested in making it different. Sometimes you may recall your dream and say, "I had a wild dream," or, "a fantastic dream," but while it's happening you take it pretty much in stride. It doesn't seem out of the ordinary, because it is ordinary on the astral dream plane to think something and to have it appear in your hand, or to imagine a place and instantly arrive at this place. Even to travel without a body is completely normal on the astral dream level. This waking dream has other conditions of existence, and when you learn to play within these boundaries, then freedom happens. When you learn to play within the rules of this particular dimension, this is mastery— and you see the miraculous magnificence of the moment called life. Sit back and enjoy the ride! It's so magnificent; it's so magical! It's your magical mystery tour that's waiting to take you away.

This is how you live your life in freedom: every moment not knowing where you're going to lay your head at night, not knowing who you're going to meet that day, and also not knowing who you're going to meet at night. Do you plan who you're going to have your dreams with at night? Do you wish, "I hope I dream that I win the lottery. I hope I dream that I get to hang out with Madonna. I hope I dream that I become the President of the United States"? You don't program your dreams! You lay your head down, you let go, and you go to sleep. Then you let yourself be surprised by whatever dream arises. It's the same in this dream, my love! Every moment a new dream is available, a new dream lover, and a new dream problem. It's all a dream. Don't get stuck in identifying with any of it; then you're in your dead mind again, holding on or pushing away. Just be open and available to this moment, which is always changing and always the same. Imagine living your life this way, not knowing who you are! Not knowing where you're going and letting Existence guide you.

Everything appears and disappears without you doing anything, like a dream. Life is but a dream, so all you have to do is merrily, merrily, merrily, merrily float down the river of Existence. It's this simple! This is the key to peace and happiness. You let go of every idea of who you're supposed to be or what you're supposed to do to be happy, to be spiritual, to be successful, to be worthy. You let it go. You discover in this moment what the truth is. It's not my truth; it's not ego's truth. It's truth without ego, without past and without future, without time. It's not even the present, if the present is held in time. It's now. Now is always, and this is who you are, this now. The forms are constantly changing, but you are the formless dreamer. You remain the same, as the dream constantly changes.

Although the dream continues until it's over, and a new dream may arise and play itself out, it is of no consequence because you've realized who you are. The dream is rising and falling within you. Nothing is happening to you. Nothing can happen to you, because it's all happening within you. This whole dream rises from your unconscious. Be conscious of this truth. This unconscious is the creative impulse. It's what allows your life to happen, to unfold. Everything that happens in your life rises from this unconscious that you are. Become conscious of the unconscious, of the vast resource that you are, the endless Source of your own Self. This Consciousness is the unconscious. If it is known, if it is conscious, it is mind. It's what you already know. Been there, done that. It's what you already understand about yourself. It's the limited thought that you hold yourself to be. The unconscious is the unmanifest, the unknown; this is the true Consciousness that you all are.

Don't postpone your awakening one second more! Wake up to the unconscious and bring it to Consciousness. This means: identify with that which is unknown, the mystery, the unmanifest. If it is known, it's past. The unknown is present. You discover in this moment what is truth, now. It's not a concept. It's not an idea. It's not a philosophy. It's not an opinion. It's a direct abidance in the unknown, the unconscious Consciousness that you are, this God-Realization. You are already That; become conscious of it now by dropping what is known. Drop all of your ideas about yourself, where you've been and where you're going, and simply be still. In this stillness, the unconscious becomes conscious. In this stillness, it is seen directly that you are already That. There's nothing to do. Be still. This moment, this precious moment, is stillness itself—when you just stop projecting into the future or looking over your shoulder into the past, and you let yourself be here now.

This "I," this personality you've believed yourself to be your whole lifetime, is nothing but a thought. You access a memory from it and say, "I am this person; I have this history," but it's just a story! It's not happening now. You access it and you pretend it's happening now. You say, "Well, I drove here in a car," or, "I was born," or, "I had a relationship," or, "I suffered." It's all concept. In this moment, there is only Consciousness creating your experience through your mind. Everything comes from mind—even your emotions come from mind. You wouldn't experience this body if you didn't have mind, and you wouldn't experience emotion if you didn't have mind. All emotions come from thought; whatever it is, it starts as a thought. This body starts as a thought; these feelings start as thought, so pay no attention to what you think or what you feel. Give full permission to the body. Give full permission to the emotions, but don't get stuck in them.

Feelings come and go like weather. The anger comes, the sadness comes, the laughter comes and goes, and there is no one to resist it. If you don't resist it, it doesn't stick around. You know that old saying, "What you resist persists?" When there is no one to indulge it, it just comes and goes. Who is saying that this moment of emotion is more valid than a moment of no emotion? It's all mind. If you're somebody who's done a lot of emotional release work or therapy, it might seem like denial when you finally say, "Enough. I'm fed up. I'm gonna stop acting out. I'm gonna see what happens if I just stay quiet right here." Don't deny your feelings if they're flowing, but there's no need to indulge them either. If the energy is moving, direct it—it's just energy. Emotion is just energy. Redirect it. Every time your sexual energy rises does not mean you have to have sex; you can redirect it. Do the same thing with your emotions, and then you become the master of them.

Everything that is happening to you in your life is divine order. It's all designed to wake you up from this wonderful dream. Every moment in this dream has led you to this moment now. All suffering, all struggle, all effort, all doubt, all despair, and all pain has led you to this moment of awakening. Here and now, wake up! Be still enough to wake up and see the truth: you are awakeness itself. You are Awareness, pure Awareness. It's this simple! Everything that has happened to you up until this moment has just been a dream. When you see that who you have believed yourself to be, is nothing more than a conglomerate of memories and mental constructs, when you can see that it doesn't exist except as a memory, you can drop it. When you can see that it is not real, this idea of who you hold yourself to be can easily fall away. If you still believe in it, if you still have investment in it, if you still hold it as real, how can you possibly drop it? If you find what you think is a diamond, you carry it with you; you hold it dear. But if somebody tells you it's only cubic zirconium, you don't have to carry it with you anymore. You can give it away, or you don't mind if you lose it.

One of the reasons we sit in silence before satsang is to clear our minds of any ideas. Any expectations, any concepts, any understandings, and any beliefs, you just drop them all in the silence and be as empty as possible. Satsang demagnetizes your minds. It clears them so that you can have a fresh start in this moment; you can begin fresh and new in this moment with no history, no herstory. A beginner's mind: innocent, empty, with infinite possibility. Don't cling to your memories; let them go. No memory is valuable. Don't cling to your dreams and your hopes and your desires; let them go, they're worthless. Stay empty, stay available, and don't collect memories. Don't store anything. It's like the food that goes through your body: you eat it, you use it and you dispose of it, you don't keep it. You do it with your clothing: you wear it, it wears out, you dispose of it, you throw it away or give it away. You do it with everything in your life, except for your thoughts! You keep your thoughts stored up in a trunk inside your attic someplace. "Maybe I'll need them one day, these are important memories, I have to value them, I have nothing else." Then there's no room. Clean out your attics, demagnetize your minds, and return to Emptiness.

Stop referencing yourself to your past. Your past did not happen. Listen to me: whatever you believed happened in the past did not happen! It's just a dream! The abuse in your childhood did not happen. The neglect did not happen. The joy did not happen. None of it happened! Do you hear me? You are dreaming, and you're believing you had a past; you're believing you're somebody. This is the truth: it did not happen! There is only this moment; today did not even happen. Only this moment—the rest is a dream. It's a dream that you're keeping alive as a memory in your mind. It's concept, and this concept keeps you from living fully alive in this moment. You must see this if you want to be free.

There is no past; there is no future. There's only this moment, but you hold the concept of the past and then it keeps you from being alive here and now. You are free, my love; you are totally free! You are free Consciousness, and you are deluding yourself that you have a past, that you have an identity, that you're a person that came from somewhere and is going somewhere. Hear these words, even if they do not make sense to your mind. Hear these words: the past did not happen, no matter how good, no matter how terrible, it's just a dream. Drop your point of view; drop your frame of reference. Don't come from anywhere and don't go anywhere, just be here. Just keep still, and you will see the freedom of your own Self in this moment. Don't keep your stories alive, in your therapy and in your conversations, in your relationships and in your ambitions. Die to this past. Free yourselves!

Thought is past. Don't identify with thought when it rises. Don't believe your mind. It's hard not to think in this world, but you can ignore your thoughts. You can simply witness them without identifying. Keep quiet. This is what we're here for; this is all we're here for. Empty your mind of whatever you may be clinging to; empty it. Wash it clean. Satsang is like the Ganga River in India: it purifies your mind on your way to the ocean of God. You sit here and you're purified of all the old thoughts and beliefs, ideas, concepts, aversions, and desires. They just fall away into the ocean of Emptiness. You're left here free of all of that, free of all those future postponements and past regrets. In this freedom, here you are—it's obvious. In this freedom, it's here and now. So let your mind be quiet, let it empty itself of all concepts. Whatever thoughts you carry, whatever thoughts you hold is what you attract in your life. If you hold negative thoughts, you may have a negative experience. If you hold positive thoughts, you may have a positive experience—but if you hold no thought, you have a pure experience before thought, and the mystery reflects you.

The unmanifest reflects you and becomes manifest in the moment of watching it, and it can change in that next second. Don't cling to anything, and it can change in that next second. No matter how horrible it may be, it can move—and you find yourself completely washed clean by the spring rain. The same is true for the sunshine. Don't become attached to this either, because in the next moment the clouds come in. Simply sit in total enjoyment of this life that you're creating without attachment to any of it. As Papaji used to say, "Enjoy everything, but cling to nothing." Cling to absolutely nothing, don't know who you are moment by moment, don't make conclusions, don't put limitations on yourself, just be open and available. See that everything is perfect, just the way it is. There cannot be a moment that is not perfect. So what do you do when you realize this perfection? What is there to do but sing and dance and share love? Let your mouth open, and music comes out! The song of silence. The dance of Emptiness.

How can I talk about Emptiness? Close your eyes. Disappear. Emptiness is; it's self-evident. You don't have to do anything to make it happen. In fact, the more you do, the further you move from it. Like a fly trying to get out of flypaper, the more you struggle, the more stuck you get. The more you try to obtain realization or the more you try to wake up, the more identified you become with the one who wants to wake up. Who wants to wake up? Let this one go. It's just your mind. You're already awake! Empty your mind and realize it! Emptiness is not something. Emptiness is the absence of everything. It's the Source of who you are. You come from nothing and you return to nothing, and this moment of something that you call your life is a wonderful creation to be celebrated—but don't be attached to it, because it comes and goes in the blink of an eye. The moment you're looking for it, you miss the next moment that comes. Be empty, my love.

Do you really want to wake up and stop dreaming? What will remain then? You say, "Nothing." People toss this word around like it means something, but it's just another concept: "nothing," "no one," "emptiness." No one is no one. Emptiness is the absence of everything. The closest approximation you can have to it is when you're in deep sleep and there is no memory, no dream, nothing. Is this what you want? This is what most atheists believe happens when you die! Some of them welcome it; others fear it. The body dies, it's buried in the ground, and what remains? Nothing, absolutely nothing. There is no heaven, there is no hell, there is no God. Nothing remains of this lifetime. Is that what you want? Be truthful with yourselves; or is it that you just want to fulfill your dream?

This "I" cannot be in Emptiness. The "I" who has an experience disappears in Emptiness. If there's still an "I" having an experience, it's not Emptiness; it's an experience of emptiness, and that comes and goes. The "I" experiences emptiness, and then the "I" experiences something in the way of emptiness. The "I" experiences stuck-ness, or the "I" experiences ecstasy, or the "I" experiences insight or wisdom or enlightenment. This is not Emptiness; there's still an "I." Inquire, "Who is experiencing?" and follow the "I" back to its Source, back to Emptiness. In truth every experience is empty, only your "I," the experiencer, thinks it's not, thinks that this experience is somehow more valid than that one. This experience is more special, that experience is horrible, don't want to do that again—this is all mind! Let the mind fall back into Emptiness, and keep quiet.

Even when you're on a train going somewhere, realize that the train car is the destination. Whether you're sitting at the station or traveling many miles per hour through the countryside—the train car, where you are, is the destination. It's celebrating where you are now that is freedom; it's accepting totally who and what you are right now. It's realizing that you don't really go anywhere, that there's nowhere to go. Sometimes the train is going uphill, sometimes through a mountain pass, and sometimes it gets stuck. Through it all, you're sitting in the car, enjoying the moment. The landscapes are passing by, and you're watching faces of people watching the train. Sometimes they're a blur, and sometimes the train stops and their gaze meets yours, and there's a connection. Sometimes they get on the train and share the cabin with you for a while, sometimes they may even share the bunk with you, and then they leave and you keep going. But you always know that the destination has already been reached before you even left the station on this eternal journey from here to here.

Stillness has no quality. This is a great misunderstanding of the mind, thinking that stillness has a particular flavor to it, a particular quality. It does not. It doesn't mean you sit in a cave all day; it doesn't mean you are always peaceful; it doesn't mean there's never a reaction. Stillness means that your focus always remains here. You don't leave here. You remain here; that's what it means to be still. You don't move. Your mind rises, your emotions respond, but you don't move with them. You stand still and watch them. It's like a parade; you don't have to join the parade and beat the drum, and dance and sing and protest. You stand on the sidelines and watch the protesters go by, watch the entertainment dance past. You no longer have to be the center of attention; you're just as happy sitting still and watching the parade go by.

You know you're ready to be still when you're not so interested in your story, what you're feeling, what you're thinking—when you're not trying to figure it out. You're ready to keep still, and that means whatever story rises, falls away by itself, because you don't pick it up. This is what happens in freedom. You lose interest in your story. And sometimes, because you aren't interested in the stories of your friends and neighbors, your friends and neighbors lose interest in you! Who cares? Freedom is a solo journey. This is the greatest paradox of all, my love. Freedom is a journey alone. You go alone. You realize yourself alone, and when you realize, you see that we are all-one! We were never alone to begin with—but you have to be willing to go alone.

Once you get the knack of stillness, then you can be available to your own life. You can just simply live in freedom. And you can play full-on: be as emotional as you like, be as physical as you like, let the desires come and go. Let them be fulfilled or not, and it doesn't touch you. Certain emotions will play themselves out, desires will finish, certain aversions will fall away, but the essence of your conditioning will remain. It takes a lot of effort to change your conditioning, and who wants to change your conditioning but your conditioning? Who else wants to change your mind but your mind? Be still first. When you are shifting gears from reverse to forward, you have to come to neutral first. You have to come to a standstill. Just be still. Don't know who you are; be open and available and then watch the grace of your own Self take over.

If you spend your whole life searching for a partner, when you find the person who you think is the one, then you're still. You stop searching. When you think you've found the one, you stop looking. In that moment you say, "I have found the one. My search is over," and then you are still, then you are silent. So see that the one you are searching for is right in front of you. It's your own Self. You are the One! There is no other. There is no relationship except with Self, and whomever you're playing partners with is only a reflection. There is no other. There is only one of us. When there is a fight, you are fighting with yourself. Make peace with yourself. Look into what it is that's engaging you and then drop it. Don't point the finger out there. Keep it focused on yourself. There is no out there. There's no other. You are the One.

Every interaction is with your own Self; it is your mind projected outward. You think that these forms are real! You think that this world you've created is real, and you're running around, trying to get fulfilled in it. It's just a dream! Everything that happens rises in your Consciousness. It's all a product of your imagination. You're only imagining your beloved. You are only imagining that you're married. You are only imagining that your wife is cheating on you. You are only imagining that you are getting a divorce. Nothing is really happening! This is just a dream. There's only one Consciousness, and That's who you are. Everything else is appearance and disappearance, smoke and mirrors. As long as you believe that this dream is real, it will appear as if you are not free, but even that is an illusion.

When you're free, it doesn't mean you can't be in a relationship. You can still play the game of relationship if it is in support of your freedom. Make your criteria for a relationship somebody who is going to challenge you and reflect you in freedom, someone else who is also married to truth, who will inspire you to go deeper and deeper into Self-realization. Make your partner a reflection of the master, accepting him or her however he or she is; knowing if you have a problem with it, it's your problem. It becomes what is called your *sadhana,* or your practice, and it's a great practice. To practice being at peace when your buttons are pushed by your lover, this is a great practice! If you're attached to anything, suffering will result. Sometimes the practice is to walk away, to be discriminating enough to discern whether this relationship is disturbing your peace or not. Is it in the way of my love for truth? Is my mind attached and hoping that this relationship will work so I won't have to face my loneliness? Will I get sexual pleasure? Will I fulfill my romantic inclinations? Whatever it is that pulls you, drop it and be available to the love that you already are.

I am often asked whether you can have a monogamous relationship and still live in the moment. How can I make a commitment to be monogamous? How do I know what my future will be? I could say "yes" in this moment, "I want to marry you, and we will be exclusive," and then the next moment somebody else shows up, and I want to be with that other person. What about respect for my partner? Where does it leave the other person who is wanting to be monogamous? Monogamy may appear to be contradictory to freedom, on the surface. If you believe that freedom is being able to do whatever you want in the moment, then monogamy will look like it's standing in the way of it, but this is not necessarily so. If you are monogamous with your Self first, it doesn't matter if you're reflecting with the same person every day, or a different person. Even though it appears you're with the same person, day in and day out, it is not the same person. It's a new reflection each moment, a whole different reflection of the same Self that you always are. This is how you keep a monogamous relationship fresh.

The idea that monogamy is not freedom—because freedom is to be able to have sex with whomever you want in every moment—is a misunderstanding. To think that a one-on-one relationship is any more sacred than making love with a total stranger is also a story. You only know your partner in time, and time is mind. In truth, you can love a total stranger in the moment and never see each other again. It is possible, on the level of absolute love that I'm speaking of. Then the whole relationship question becomes a device; the relationship is there to serve you in deepening your commitment to freedom. So, if it's a challenge to stay, then stay and work through your aversion. If you're staying because you're supposed to or you're afraid to leave, then get the hell out and explore the possibilities that are open to you in the moment.

It doesn't matter whether you're in relationship with one person or many people. It doesn't matter, as long as you are monogamous with your Self, meaning as long as you are committed to freedom first. Once you're committed to freedom first, you will know in the moment whether it is your ego that wants to step out of the marriage and be with somebody else, or whether it's your ego that is hiding out in the marriage and not being completely free in the moment. Make your commitment to freedom first and let monogamy rise from that, be informed by that. For some of you, this will be very important to bust your ego identification with what you think freedom is. If you're committed to truth, you're choosing whichever commitment is going to keep you abiding in freedom. If your ego has the tendency to prowl, and you're constantly looking for something better; if you see that's your tendency, then maybe you want to try monogamy. However, if your story is you're supposed to be married, even though there's no true connection between you and your partner, then maybe it's time for you to break out. There's no rule about this.

Trust your commitment to freedom, and in the moment, you know that whatever choice is made for you is the perfect choice. There's no guilt. There's no one choosing. Stop making choices and decisions from your minds and let Existence choose for you! This is called choiceless Awareness. In this choicelessness, your karma plays itself out. Then you're watching the movie, and you don't know how it's going to end. You don't know how it ends until it ends! Some movies are so predictable, you can tell how they're going to end. Don't make your life predictable. Make your life unpredictable; be creative. Don't be a cliché.

This moment is always a surprise. You never know what's going to happen next! If you think you know, you're in your mind. You're in a projection into the future. In this moment you don't know. It's always a surprise. This is the adventure called life! This is the greatest gift of being alive: not knowing. Yet this inquiring mind wants to know; it wants to know what lurks around the corner so it can feel safe. If you listen to this mind, if you live by this mind, not only will you be safe, you'll be dead! Aliveness is the mystery when we don't know what's coming around the corner, so let yourself be surprised in each moment. It certainly makes it exciting! It teaches you to be available to whatever happens, instead of constantly using your mind to seek safety, to defend, and to protect. If you run when you're afraid and stay when you're attached, there is no fun. Absolutely none, it's no longer fun. Then life becomes work; then life becomes struggle. Then life is suffering. Then all you can do with your time is think of a way out. You spend all your time thinking of a way out of your suffering. That's a pain in a neck. That's a bad back. That's a case of cancer. That's not fun—it's struggle, it's strife, it's grief, it's depression, it's stress. Now what's fun about that?

This moment is fun! If you're not having fun in this moment, you must be in your mind. So drop this mind and celebrate at this wonderful party called "Now." We're having a party now. This party never ends, because now never ends! This moment has no beginning and no end. This moment is who you are, always changing but always the same. You will live this moment for the rest of your life if you live in the now. You don't have to worry about the future; you don't have to think about the past. This moment is fun! It's not about having fun; it's not about seeking fun; it's being fun. That's its nature. It's celebration; it's joy; it's laughter; it's freedom. Whatever is happening now, this is it! So drop the mind that doesn't want to do it, that runs away from it, that wants it to last longer, or that doesn't want it to end. This mind is in the way of fun.

Fun is being total. Fun is not minding whatever is happening now or is not happening now. This is what you're alive for, just to be in joy and bliss and love and peace. So every time this mind that wants to run away or wants to stay rises, don't mind your mind. Accept what is, whatever it is, and when your mind doesn't accept it—that's fine, don't mind it. Let it bitch on its own, let it complain, let it have the impulse to run away, but don't run away. Let it long to stay with your beloved forever, but when forever goes away, when the beloved walks away, wish him well. The form comes and goes but not who you are, not the essence, not the love, not the joy. When you recognize it, life is your playground; it's so much fun to create, to dance, to share, to love, to serve, to make whoopee! Whoopee is when there is no mind. Whoopee is when you can laugh at whatever happens, no matter what the loss is, no matter what the gain is. You can laugh when you lose your lover, you can laugh when you gain 50 pounds— and then you laugh again when you lose 50 pounds and you get another lover! You laugh at the loss and you laugh at the gain, because who you are isn't touched by it. Who you are is eternal, with no beginning and no end. This is what's fun!

Nothing to do but simply be. Nowhere to go but here. Now here is always changing, but you remain the same. If you're available to it, you're never bored. It's an adventure! All you have to do is say "yes." "Yes" is freedom; "no" is mind. "No" is control, "no" is resistance, and "no" is judgment. "Yes" is whoopee! If you find yourself stuck, if your lives are stuck, just practice saying "yes" to whatever Existence throws you—and throw it right back! You don't have to hold whatever hot potato Existence throws you. Say "yes," welcome it, and throw it right back. Don't hold on to anything. Don't own anything. Don't own your house. Don't own your car. It's all on loan. Don't own your lover, your partner or your children. It's all on loan. And certainly don't own these bodies, because the minute you drive them out of the parking lot they devalue! The book value goes down by at least twenty percent! It's better to lease these bodies. Lease your bodies, then you can trade them in for a new one whenever you need to. If they get into an accident, you don't need insurance, you just get a new one. You don't have to own these bodies; you lease them from God. Now, of course, you're God, so you're just leasing them to yourself for a dollar.

Everywhere you look, you are looking at your own Self. Everyone you talk to, you are talking to your own Self. This is God! Yes? God is everywhere. We learned this at school. So this is who you are, you are God. It is time to take this simple recognition to heart and live from this truth. You are God; you have no beginning and no end. This is the truth, but you dream that you are somebody, some little personality who is playing this game called life. Some of you have taken it so seriously that you have forgotten that it is a game! You have forgotten to have fun in the game called life. You are God, or whatever word you want to call it: Consciousness, Awareness, Love, That. We call it That so you don't have any charge on the word, but That is God. That is the Source from which all of these games rise and fall, your own being, who you are—the Oneness, which is you. This is the truth, and this is all that satsang is: you sit with someone who tells the truth and says, "Wake up; it is just a game."

Hide and go seek was over lifetimes ago; what are you doing still hiding? Come on, let's play something else! There are so many other games to play when you wake up and realize it's a game. Ask yourself, "Am I invested in winning this game, or do I know it's just for fun?" If I know it's for fun, then I'm going to have a blast! If I am invested in winning, then I'm going to take it so seriously that the fun will be taken out of it. Knowing life is a game makes you able to play it more fully. This is being awake: remembering that life is a game and playing fully. You have seen players in the sports arena who think the game is real; you have seen athletes being paid millions of dollars to bounce balls and throw them in hoops, or hit them with wooden bats. They think it is real! It is not a game for them; they take it seriously, twenty million dollars a year seriously! There is no fun there. They are invested, and many of them are unhappy. You are happy when you wake up, and you realize life is but a game.

Drop the whole idea that there is any goal in this game. There is no goal! Recognize that it is a game, and the rest will take care of itself. Recognize that you are God playing a game. Read the *Bhagavad Gita;* read any ancient scripture and you will see this truth. You are God playing a game, and you can play any game you want. You can play the game of the lonely disciple, worshipping the high guru: "Wow, isn't this a fun game? I get to feel special the closer I get. I get to feel miserable the further I get pushed out." You can play: "I am looking for my special soul mate," and when you find the soul mate, you get a really big rush. Then the next moment, when the soul mate is looking at someone else, you feel really crushed! How about the game: "I want to amass a million; I want to make a fortune"? Wow, you feel really juiced when you get close to that goal, and then the stock market crashes and you want to jump off the ledge of a building! Whatever it is, if you are invested in the game, it is no longer fun. If you see it as a game, you have fun with it. Then you are open-hearted, you are light-hearted, you are easy-going, you are free-flowing, and you take nothing seriously.

Let yourself be amused by who you are this lifetime, because your life is an amusement park. The funny thing about amusement parks is that if you know it's an amusement park, you can have fun, but if you don't, the haunted house can be scary as hell, and the roller coaster ride, forget about it! In an amusement park, you know it's not real. You know that the haunted house has ghosts, but they're really illusions, so you can have a good time. You know the roller coaster is actually attached to a track. It appears scary, but it's really safe, so you can enjoy the ride. If you thought it was real, you'd be freaking out! It's only fun because you know it's not real. Could you imagine driving in your car a hundred miles an hour down a steep hill, around hairpin turns, and suddenly you find yourself doing a loop de loop? You'd be terrified. Your life would be passing in front of your eyes! It's only fun because you know it's not real. It's the same way in this amusement park of life. When you realize that this life is an illusion, it does not invalidate the experience or beauty of the moment, but frees you up to enjoy it and participate fully.

When we wake up and realize that life is but a dream, that's when the amusement starts to happen! That's when you can really enjoy the amusement park. Every activity you do becomes another expression of amusement, another opportunity to enjoy the moment. That's what we're here for: to live in joy. If you enjoy suffering, then it will continue. If you enjoy misery, it will continue. If you enjoy struggle, it will continue, and that's perfect. If you enjoy postponement, if you enjoy being a disciple, if you enjoy being alone—whatever you enjoy will continue, because we're here to live in joy. If you enjoy nothing then it won't continue. It won't even begin! You'll just enjoy joy for no particular reason. Joy without reason. Unreasonable joy. Unconditional joy, free of your conditioning.

Enlightenment is not serious; on the contrary, it's light and full of joy. Joy for your creation, the joy of the creator for everything that rises in your Consciousness. It's all seen as such beauty, such love, such joy! You live in joy and you enjoy everything. It just bubbles over! It's contagious: people meet you and they feel this joy, and you disappear into this joy. There's nobody left to worry, "Oh, I need more joy; I don't have enough joy." No, there's just joy. Remember how joyful we are on Christmas? This is what it's like all the time in freedom, but for absolutely no reason. Then your joy can never go away. Then your joy is always here. When the object of your joy is not important, nonexistent, the one who is attached to joy disappears too, and there's only unbridled, unconditional joy.

Trust the silence of your own heart over the noise of your mind. No matter what happens with your mind when it rises, no matter how far you may feel like you've left your joy behind, all you have to do is close your eyes and come home to the joy that you are. It's always here in this moment; this is the beauty of it. It's right here and now in the silence. Close your eyes, drop everything outside and it's right here in the silence—this joy, this unconditional joy. It's not outside of you; it's your nature. Don't forget this. Just close your eyes, and it's right here always, like a river of joy. It's always available, and every action rises from it, every word you speak is an overflow from this river. You trust it because you trust the joy, you trust the love, you trust the silence more than your mind with its fears, and desires, and aversions. Then everywhere you go there is joy, whether you're home alone or busy in the amusement park.

When you are finished with the amusement park—when you are really finished riding the roller coaster and spinning around the merry-go-round hoping to get that ring, when you're finished playing the games hoping to hit the bull's eye and win that teddy bear for your girl or guy—there's a whole other quality of life available. Are you ready to stop chasing happiness and be happiness itself? Are you ready to stop looking for love and realize yourself as love? Are you ready to stop searching for God and see the God that you are—that pure, blissful awareness which is your very nature? It's really up to you; you can hang out in the carnival for as long as you want. No one is going to make you come home; you have to decide to come home on your own.

Once you've decided to give up the carnival, to give up chasing the ring, then God, your own Self, supports your life in this direction. All that's needed is a willingness to finish, a willingness to give up the game, a willingness to stop chasing the childish desires and to keep still. Allow whatever needs to play itself out to play itself out. The haunted house may still be howling, the fun house may still be reflecting you in distorted mirror images, you might even still feel sick to your stomach once in a while, while your head stops spinning—but you keep still through all of this, you just keep still. You don't run, you don't avoid, you don't look for another ride on the merry-go-round; you just keep still. This is what it takes. Your mind will be begging you to put another quarter in the machine and take another spin. Like an addict, like a junkie, it will be begging you to go for another ride, to pick up your story once more, so that you can avoid coming home and realizing the peace that you are. This is why so few realize themselves in the carnival. This is why you don't find the Buddha in the fun house, because it's so distracting to be in the amusement park and keep still.

The only way to finish is to stop chasing and to just stand still. If you find yourself on a wild ride for a moment, and it's the same ride you've taken a million times before, ask yourself, "Do I need to do it once again?" If the answer is "no," then this is grace, even though everything in your life may be working against your realizing it. Everything—your duties, your responsibilities, your culture, your conditioning, your friends, your family; everyone and everything is telling you to keep dreaming. Keep chasing the dream, the American dream. You too can be happy! Just buy a new car, a new house, new furniture, a new wardrobe, and while you're at it, why not get a new husband? You live in a consumerist society: consume, consume, and then you'll be happy. It's up to you, whenever you're ready to stop wasting your time searching for heaven in the amusement park. Whenever you're willing to keep still, heaven is realized in that moment.

What are you still chasing? Approval from others, status in your society, satisfaction from helping, spiritual pride from achieving some type of enlightenment? What are you still chasing? Financial security, career ambitions, sex, drugs, rock 'n roll? Look, because the very thing you are chasing is keeping you from experiencing heaven right now. Many have tasted the essence of peace, true inner-peace, in satsang. Don't throw it away; stay in satsang. Nourish it; don't lose it in the crowds at the amusement park. Be quiet, stay home, celebrate your aloneness, stop chasing, and be still. Watch how freedom finds you; watch how heaven appears in front of your eyes. Watch how the love that you've always been longing for is realized as your very own Self. This is a message a long time in coming—thirty-five million years! It's up to you. When you choose to let go, to finish with the amusement park, the Self that you are will support you in every way.

You are free, that's all there is to it, and any story you tell yourself otherwise is just a story, so have fun with it! Have fun with your struggles and your sufferings and your endeavors, with your paths and your practices and your religions. Have fun with them because they're all make-believe! Everything is make-believe. Nothing is real. Rest in this truth and you are free. How much fun can we have in this realization? What celebration is available, when we recognize that everything is make-believe? The opportunity to play in this amusement park is instantly available with this simple recognition that everything is make-believe. So take nothing seriously; abide as nothing. Fall in love with nothing. Give yourself over to nothing. Desire nothing, and abide as freedom. If something rises, don't believe it—because it's nothing, too, just a momentary lapse into misidentification. It doesn't matter; it can't touch That. You can't touch That. That is spotless, beginning-less, changeless, and it's always here. This is who you are, you are always here, and though you play this game of hide and seek with yourself in misidentification, it still does not touch That. It cannot. So rest assured, you are free—even with your stories, even with your egos, even with your hopes and dreams—you are free!

Fall in Love with Truth

Fall in love with truth. Fall in love with freedom. If you are not in love with truth and freedom, then forget about it! You're wasting your time. You can come to satsang after satsang until you're blue in the face, until your butt is sore, until your knees are bleeding, but unless you're in love with truth, you won't take it home with you. It will be just another concept that your mind will keep in its misidentification, in its defense. You must fall in love with truth so totally that you disappear into it, and there is no more defense. Then all you want to do is live, breathe and eat truth; nothing else is more important! That is how you live in freedom. If not, it's very easy to come to satsang and feel good. You feel good in the presence of love, you feel good to be with your beloveds, to see me, to see each other. It's all lovely. Then you go home and your mind is rushing back in! You might pop in a tape or pick up a book, but after you put it away the mind rises again, and it appears as if your peace and love were ephemeral. It is only when you really fall in love with truth, when nothing else is more important, that you can sustain it. Fall in love and stay in love.

You must fall in love with freedom. You must desire only freedom. Nothing else can matter more! Not your job, not your lover, not even your health. Nothing can come before freedom, nothing. If something does, if freedom is second or third or fourth on your list, it will not happen. Why is it that there's only a Buddha or a Jesus every few hundred years? Why is it some people free themselves and others remain in bondage? Why is it that some of us live in love and bliss and others are in suffering? It's this desire for freedom. It's falling in love with the truth so intensely that you can never be separate from it! Once you have fallen in love with truth, it hurts too much to be away from it; you can never be without it again. Your life is pale without it. There's only suffering without it.

Freedom has to be your number one commitment. You have to be married to the truth. You can't say that I want freedom and then chase the latest hot number walking down the street. It doesn't work this way! You can't say, "I want freedom, but I want to feel good while I'm making myself available to it. I want freedom as long as it's on my terms. I want freedom if it feels good. If it starts to feel uncomfortable, I'm out of here." It doesn't work this way. Marry freedom, so that nothing is more important than freedom—nothing: no body, no relationship, no money, no prestige. Then, when you're fully committed to freedom, when you know that you and freedom are one, you can take the relationship on and play with it; you can take the job on and play with it, because you know that it's all secondary. You're already married. There may be a woman in your bed, but she's second to freedom. There may be a man asking for your hand in marriage, but you're already married to truth. Marry the truth and it'll always be here for you. It will never abandon you if you don't abandon it. Make truth your number one beloved; don't make it your mistress. Don't make it second banana; make it the top dog. Make it the master that rules your life. Surrender to it, fully, totally. This is what we all long for.

Falling in love with truth is like a first date. You're sitting in the booth over a Coke or a malted or something, just looking into each other's eyes. That's what it's all about: falling in love, looking into your own eyes, into the eyes of Self. When you fall in love with someone, all you can do is think of them, day in and day out. You even dream of them in your sleep. If you're lucky enough to have fallen in love with truth, then it is easy to call off the search, because when you fall in love, you're not looking at anybody else. Before that moment, you were shopping. You walked into a party, and you scoped it out immediately: who's in the room, who's a potential partner in the room? But once you're in love you walk in with your partner, the room disappears and you don't notice anybody. When you are in love, all you can think of is your beloved! It becomes almost obsessive. It consumes you. You can't explain why you fell in love. You can sing about it, but you can't explain it. This is what it takes for freedom, this kind of vigilance. You are so in love with truth, you are so in love with freedom, you are so in love with God that you offer up your whole life to this end. Everything else takes second priority. This is the only way you can live in freedom sustainably. It's not a casual relationship!

Fall in love with Self and offer up your life to God. Then watch how God uses you, watch how your life blossoms as a result of this surrender. You fall in love, and you say, "God, I give you this life. This life is not for me. This life is not for this ego. This life is yours. Make me an instrument of your peace, my Lord. I marry you. I'm yours, take me. I offer myself up, in love, in surrender." You don't have to worry about a thing. Everything from this point on is taken care of. Everything. It may not look the way your bachelor mind expects it, the way your single self, your separate self, wants it. It may not look this way, but the Master whom you're now married to, the Lord at whose feet you have surrendered, your true Self, has now taken over. Everything is happening in divine order. Can you trust that? If you can, then it's fun from this moment on. No matter what happens, trust that it always is perfect. Then you can have fun; you can relax and enjoy the ride.

Fall in love, my sweet. Don't be afraid to fall in love, to lose yourself in this love—so that you can't think of your own needs anymore, so your own needs are not important. So that everything you do is an expression of and an expression to Self, a gift of and a gift to Self. This is the message of satsang. You are already Self. This is true, but to realize this truth can be an arduous and difficult journey. People have lost their minds on this journey. Fall in love with Self, and let Self guide you. Don't trust your minds, trust Existence—and when the mind rises and wants to do something, do nothing. Do absolutely nothing! Keep still, keep quiet and don't touch it, don't touch the mind, no matter what. This is vigilance. This is how you sustain freedom. This is how you serve Self. When you don't touch the mind, you are an empty vessel. Self is free to move through you as an instrument of peace, an empty bamboo that plays Krishna's beautiful melody for everyone to hear. You are not in the way with your silly needs and desires and worries and fears. There is only the song of pure Consciousness.

We are all *bhaktas.* We are lovers of truth, yet we don't know what truth is. How can you know what truth is? You cannot know. Truth can only be known when you are not here, when you are not in the way. You can conceptualize truth, you can try to understand truth, and you can make truth a distant goal that you want to attain, but you can't know truth. Truth is realized when you are not. But love—this is something we all have experienced, we're born as love. Look at a baby—you have only to look at a baby to see this pure love. Then the ego develops, and what does the ego learn how to do? It learns how to defend against love. What do we tell our children? Don't talk to strangers; be careful, the world is not safe. What happens to this pure love? It disappears; it's squelched under the heavy foot of the mind. You were born as love, and then you lost this love when ego rose and became afraid and felt itself as separate. Then you spent the rest of your life looking for love in all the wrong places, outside of yourself. You became beggars, looking for love and terrified to find it, because somehow you knew that if you really found love, you would disappear in that moment. This is what happens when you meet love; you disappear!

Fall in love with truth. Fall in love with God. Stop resisting. See that your whole life is perfect and is revealing itself moment by moment in perfection. Any moment that you see as imperfect is your misguided mind. It's not the truth; it's just your perception in that moment. This whole existence is perfect just the way it is. Trust this more than your mind! Trust the love of your heart. Fall in love. Fall in love so that your mind disappears into this love, immersed like a wave back into the ocean. This is the most direct path; this is how you stay in freedom. Don't postpone. Make this important. Make freedom your number one priority! Let yourself fall in love. Let yourself disappear into love. It's the most direct path. If you let yourself fall in love totally, then you as you know yourself to be will disappear. This is what happens in love. If you fall in love, this "I" just disappears organically. So don't hold back; let this "I" disappear into this pool of love that you are.

You are afraid of love. You search for it, but you fear it at the same time. This is the conflict; this is why the world is the way it is. Give yourself to love. Love totally, as if this is your last moment to love! Love everyone. Love your enemies, love your friends, love strangers; love family, love your employees, love your bosses. Just love. Love God everywhere, and disappear into this love until you do not remain, until there's no more "I," there's only love. This is what you long for! How do I know this? Because you're my own Self. Do you really know what freedom is? Maybe you've tasted it for a second when there was no mind. But you know what love is: it's your very nature; it's who you are. It's who breathes and who dances, who eats and who moves and who sleeps. You can sit there in your minds, trying to understand, but until you fall in love, you will never recognize freedom, because there will still be an "I" that separates itself. It says, "I am free," or "I understand," or "I am nothing; I am emptiness." There's still somebody saying something—but in love there's nobody, there's only love. You've all experienced it. Making love, you disappear in that one second. I say disappear forever into love! Fall in love. It's like a death. There's no more you and I; there's only love. Don't be afraid of love; it's what you long for.

L et yourself disappear. People think that the spiritual path is about finding yourself. In truth, it's about losing yourself, disappearing into That. Whoever you have believed yourself to be, whatever limitations you have placed on yourself disappear in satsang. They can't hold up to the truth. There's no way the lie can hold up; there's no way the illusion can hold up to reality. It disappears. So let yourself disappear in satsang, like a bubble ready to pop. Remember being a child, blowing bubbles? Each one was so unique, so different—some big, some small, floating, catching the light, playful. Then "Pop!" Finished. Back to nothing. This is who you are as form; you're just a bubble. For that moment when you believe yourself to be the bubble, you think you're limited. But when you pop, what remains is nothing. Where's the parameter that was holding the air in this sphere? It's gone! You become all the air. You become the sky itself, the vastness of the sky—but in Truth you always were. There was just a thin veil that made it look like you were separate. This veil was destined to pop. It couldn't last. These bodies, these bubbles, these containers—they don't last. These lives that have bubbled up from Consciousness, they don't last. When the pop happens, the realization of this Oneness that has always been is seen clearly. The air that's in the bubble is the same air that surrounds the bubble. It's all the same air.

Disappear into thin air. Once you've realized yourself as air, you can form any bubbles you want! You blow the bubbles! You fill them with your Self in all forms. You see them in your body; you see them in other bodies; you see them in every body. You see yourself as air, this air that is your own Self in all bodies. It's so beautiful, so many bubbles! The reason we come to satsang is to realize this Oneness that we are, to disappear into it, to merge back into That. It happens so effortlessly! The bubble pops in satsang. You close your eyes, and whoever you have imagined yourself to be simply disappears. Everything falls away and nothing remains. This nothing is seen clearly as your very nature. This nothing with no limitations, no parameters, pure formlessness, infinite possibility, with no beginning and no end: this is who you are. Once you realize this, it's so much fun to play with the bubbles! It's so much fun to watch the forms rise and fall. It's so much fun to be the creator, creating these forms. Sometimes it's a big bubble, sometimes it's a little bubble, sometimes it's many little bubbles; but remember you are always the air. Don't let the bubbles fool you.

You minus you equals God. When there is no you, then there is God. All of your searching, all of your techniques are for this experience of disappearing. When you make love you disappear; when you meditate you disappear—when you dance, the dancer becomes the dance and you disappear; you merge. When you have a peak experience, in that peak moment you disappear. This is what we all long for, yet the irony is that you can't seek disappearing, because the one who is seeking is the one who has to disappear. You can't make disappearing happen. It's one of those accidents, an ultimate accident, when the "I" merges back into silence. You feel it in satsang; you feel it in those moments when there is no separation between observer and observed, doer and what's being done. There is no duality; there is no me and no you. There is just One.

When the "I" disappears, you merge, and then from that merging another "I" emerges to create your life, to create this moment, to create whatever your experience is. Let that "I" disappear too. Let the One who is creating the experience disappear; let the experiencer disappear. Then you are fresh again. The highest experience is when everything disappears. Even God. Until this happens, you will continue to be reborn. So forget everything, even forgetting! Forgetting and remembering belong to the mind. If you believe that you wake up, get it, and then lose it—this is all mind. Truth does not come and go. It is the constant that remains when mind disappears. You are this truth. You are the essence that does not disappear. Find it. You are That which remains, when mind is not. Find it, here now.

There is no continuity in ego; it just appears that way. There is only a thought rising from Emptiness and falling back into Emptiness. It's the misidentification with this thought as who you are that starts all of your problems; then there is trouble, then there is suffering. Let this "I" disappear—each time it rises, let it disappear again. It happens by itself if you don't cling, if you don't grasp, if you don't identify with it. The moment blossoms, and it dies. It opens and it closes, it begins and it finishes in the experience called "life." It's constantly reinventing itself. Don't have any continuity between the experiences. This is how you abide in merging. Whatever emerges from this merging is not seen as yourself, but as a thought rising in yourself, an expression of yourself, a momentary note of music or a splash of paint on a canvas. It's just a momentary expression of yourself, and it's constantly changing. Let it merge and emerge and merge again.

Let everything you do take you deeper and deeper into the silence from which the action arises. The dancer becomes the dance, the cook becomes the cooking, and the driver becomes the driving. There is no separation between you and the act. The surfer becomes the surf. You merge, this is the secret. You don't have to figure it out; you don't have to learn it; you don't have to read it in a book. You just have to be total in each moment and let go. Have no idea how the moment is supposed to turn out. Don't grasp it, don't control it—just let go. Ride the wave, let it carry you, don't force it, don't push it. Become one with it. You just disappear, and then you realize you are already one with it. Once you've tasted disappearing, in that moment you know the Source. Then abide as Source in all activities and don't get caught up in any activity.

When you merge and disappear into the Oneness and abide as Source, then it's easy to see everyone and everything as a reflection of that Source. You see it everywhere. Who is this Source? You are this Source. Who are you seeing? A reflection of yourself. If a reflection that is full of judgment comes back to you, don't believe that reflection, just love that reflection totally. You tickle it to death! You don't believe its story. Once you've dropped your own story, you don't believe anybody else's. How can you? They're your own Self! If you believe them, you're believing your own story.

When you fall in love with truth, have no more room in your heart for any of your stories, any of your beliefs, or any of your doubts. They fall away instantly. Your heart cracks open and you say, "Yes, this is it! This moment is it. Nothing else." You look into a mirror, into a million mirrors, and they all reflect back this love, this overflow, no matter what the mirror says. If there's no doubt here, there's no doubt there. We are mirrors for each other. If there is somebody you don't like, you judge your own Self. If there is somebody you admire, you admire your own Self. Everybody is a mirror. It doesn't mean you have to play with everyone; you can be discriminating. You're creating it as you go along. You're the creator. You don't have to engage with every thought that rises within your Consciousness—hopefully, you engage with none! Who you are is the absolute, the Source from which all of these reflections rise. So don't get caught up in reflections, no matter how wonderful or how horrible. It will pass, no matter what.

Your whole world is nothing but a mirror. It is a mirror reflecting who you are, and this is the truth, because there is only One. So, if there appears to be two, it is because you are looking in a mirror. Sometimes you stand in front of the bathroom mirror when you wake up in the morning, and it looks like there are two of you in the tiny little bathroom, but there is only one. Then, if you have a mirror in the door behind you, reflecting itself infinitely—this is the world! All these mirrors looking into mirrors, and there are myriad reflections. This is all we are: there is only one of us, pure Consciousness, God. And when God is looking into a mirror, this is called creation. Whatever you perceive in this mirror is your creation. No matter what is reflected back, abide in the source of the reflection. It is too easy to get distracted and caught up in the reflection. As beautiful as this creation may be, or as difficult as this creation may be, it distracts us from the Source. We forget who we are, and we think we are the mirror image! We are looking in all of these mirrors, trying to find out who we are, running around, trying to get approval from our own image. What is the reflection constantly telling you? If you believe you are not good enough, what are the reflections going to tell you? Come home to the Source. Whenever you find yourself distracted out there, in some concept of who is out there, just drop the concept and disappear back to the Source.

When you disappear, the mirror has no image. It is an empty mirror, and when it's an empty mirror, you can see clearly. It's like wiping the fog off the mirror after a hot shower. You can see clearly now. When the mirror is empty, you can clearly see that there is no one really here. It is just a blank mirror. But even when there is no one, even when there is no reflection, there is still pure Awareness reflecting Emptiness. Then images come and go in this looking glass, but nobody is identified with them. They are constantly changing, as reflections do. This is the nature of reflection, of form. It is constantly changing—but Awareness, the one who is watching the whole thing, the one who abides in the Emptiness, remains the same. There is no one who cares looking back in the mirror. Then it is perfect, each and every time. No matter who shows up, it is perfect.

Look and see yourself sitting where I am sitting. I am your mirror. I am here to reflect you in truth. That is why I sit here. I am here to reflect you in the truth of who you are. Once you have recognized who you are, you become a mirror for others; you reflect the truth of who they are. Then it is satsang wherever you go, simply reflecting the truth of who you are. Everybody you see in your daily life is merely a reflection of who you are. If you are caught up in concepts and thoughts, then they are reflecting your mind. These are called projections. You are projecting on your lover; you are projecting on your children; you are projecting on your parents. You think you see them clearly, but you cannot, for how can you see them clearly when all you see is your own mind projecting? Jesus used to say, "How can you remove a speck of sawdust from someone else's eye before you take the plank of wood out of your own?" This is projection, this plank of wood. You think you are seeing the other, but you are not. You are only seeing your mind's projection.

You are all mirrors! I look and I see my own Self, in beauty and in grace, in love, in truth. My own Self. I do not believe your projections about yourself and I do not believe your projections about me. None of it! I only see my own reflection. I only see the truth of who I am shining in your eyes. You can't hide from the truth of who you are in satsang. It's self-evident you are my own Self. There are not two; there is only one of us. Whatever you may believe and whatever I may believe is irrelevant, because you and I do not exist except as a belief. In this non-existence we meet, and some call this love—but if you still believe you are an "I" and you're looking at somebody else sitting here, then our meeting is impossible. Then all we can have is polite conversation or some kind of exchange, or maybe even some kind of meaningful connection, but it will go away. Whatever or whoever you perceive as other will go away. This is the source of all suffering, this impermanence. The minute there is an "I" who's looking to meet a "you" out there, you set yourself up for suffering. Be finished with this "I," and with it, the "you" disappears as well. Then there is only one of us.

When I look out at my Self, I see myself free and clear and full of love. I see my Self as That. I don't see somebody who needs to do something to realize That. I see my Self as That, as already realized. All I'm here to do is to reflect you in this truth, and if you're open and available, this reflection takes hold. This reflection fits like Cinderella's glass slipper—and suddenly now, instead of being a pauper sweeping ashes, you dance at the ball! You celebrate! After lifetimes of pursuing, of wanting more, of thinking you should do it better, of worshipping God outside of yourself—it can be seen, free and clear, that you're already That. You're already perfect. This is how you come to satsang. You don't come to satsang broken, and get fixed. You come to satsang already whole. Maybe you don't know it, maybe you think otherwise, but in satsang you can start where most people finish. You can start having already graduated. You can start at the end of your journey.

I'm not the man who sits in satsang to answer questions for you. I have nothing to tell you! I'm the man who mirrors you. I'm the man in the mirror who reflects you in the truth of who you are. If some ego trip rises that gets in the way of this pure mirroring, I reflect that too. I do this so that you can learn to reflect yourself. Be honest with yourself in your daily lives, so that when you see your mind rise, you can drop it. Beware. Be aware enough so you can drop it, whatever the story is that takes you out of the silence of freedom, the peace of your own heart. You know your own stories. You have tasted freedom; you've tasted suffering. What story can you possibly tell yourself that can take you out of freedom? What story is more important than abiding in the peace and love and joy of your true nature? It's easy to come to satsang and be reflected in who you are. You are love; you are pure Consciousness; you are Self. But to be reflected in who you are not—your arrogance, your selfishness, your fear—is also just as useful in the dropping of the "I" and all its stories that stand in the way. But you can only listen to that kind of feedback from someone you trust.

I am not here to reflect you as "I." I am blank. I am a blank screen in which you reflect. This is because I am not identified with "I." You are also a blank screen. There's only one blank screen here, the One. So, drop this "I." See that you are nothing; you are a blank screen, and anyone that projects on you doesn't touch you, because you are a blank screen. It doesn't matter if they like you; it doesn't matter if they hate you. You are no longer looking for approval from your mirrors. You are no longer trying to get someone to stay with you or to get someone to leave you; there is no "I" who cares anymore. This is love; this is availability; this is freedom. This is blankness. Blankness is not boring. It is nothingness, and it includes everything. It's constantly reflecting back and forth in love, with whoever shows up to reflect you. What a dance! You're available to love them all, to love each and every reflection as your own Self.

I am here to reflect you in Emptiness, and if somebody rises, I tell you. I tell you the truth! Who is this "I" who cares? Who is this "I" who is afraid? If you're sitting there, feeling comfortable, having a good time, enjoying the show, getting high, feeling love, and not being vigilant when your "I" rises, then it's just another escape. Satsang becomes another escape, another avoidance of the final dropping of your misidentification with "I." You finally realize that you, as you've known yourself to be, do not exist except as concept. Until you recognize this—until you cut all of your chasing and pursuing and avoiding, and really let yourself drop and not know who you are in the Emptiness of this moment—until you recognize this; you cannot really know who you are.

When the "I" thought rises, see the thought and do not identify with it. Drop it and tell the truth; always tell the truth. This is how you abide in freedom. Always tell the truth, no matter what the consequences are, tell the truth. Only the ego needs to lie; the truth will set you free. We're speaking of the moment by moment truth in your daily awareness. Don't hide; don't lie; don't deny; this is all ego. Each time you hide, each time you lie, each time you deny—you are making your ego more powerful, you are making it more real. Expose yourself; challenge yourself; see where you're stuck. Then in your daily life you can watch this "I" rise. You can be vigilant and watch the "I" rise so that you are not the "I." If you watch it, you're not it; you're the Awareness in which it rises— but if you don't watch it, you're identified with it, and the identification with the "I," no matter how beautiful it is, leads to suffering. You're here to wake up and see the truth of who you are, before mind rises, during the mind's activity, and after mind returns to Self. Abide in the truth, no matter what your mind tells you. Be honest with yourself, and when you feel yourself attached, inquire, bust it, and drop it. When you feel yourself getting lost in desire, you just have to let it go. When it comes, it comes, when it doesn't, it doesn't, who cares but mind? When you feel yourself identified with a point of view and you catch yourself, drop the point of view and laugh at it.

As they say in the twelve-step program, we're only as sick as our secrets. Tell the truth, stop hiding, don't deny. If ego rises, see it, admit it! Don't try to be spiritual; don't try to be free. Don't have a concept of what enlightenment is and then try and meet it; just be aware. If you see mind rise, be aware—don't deny, tell the truth! Desire is rising; anger is rising; jealousy is rising; what to do? It's all happening by itself. Thoughts are rising and falling, but to pretend they're not there—there's no freedom, there's just a thought on top of a thought on top of a thought. Until you really embrace your sinner, how can you be a saint? Until you really are willing to accept all aspects of your humanity, how can you transcend them? Then you are lopsided. There's one side of you trying to be sweet and beautiful, but what about the pungent and ugly side? There's no transcendence; there's only repression. There's only denial. Freedom is when you accept both, when you accept the good and the bad. As long as you're chasing the good and denying the bad, there's no freedom.

We hide in all kinds of ways. We hide through shame and we hide through arrogance. We hide through doubt and we hide through knowing. We hide through humor and we hide through shyness. We hide through different masks called "personality" that we wear. It is wonderful to wear them, but don't hide behind them! It's like a costume party where everybody knows it's a mask. If somebody doesn't like you, they only do not like your mask, and it doesn't matter because you are not this personality mask. When you realize this, you can stop hiding. You can be your Self.

There truly is no separation between you and the other. There is truly only One, and it is you. You're the One. As soon as "I" rises, you think that you're two, but when you drop this "I," you return to One. When you drop the "I" who likes something and dislikes something else, when you drop the "I" who desires one thing and has an aversion to another, when you drop the "I" who seeks pleasure and avoids pain, the two become One. When the "I" observes something outside of himself as an object, then there is someone who perceives an object. Suddenly, there is an "I" and an object. So be vigilant—drop the "I." Remain as One.

What is it that creates this sense of other, of separation? What is the tendency to fragment? It's usually referred to as mind. Let's call it the judging mind. This is what fragments the wholeness into pieces, because we always start with "I am." I am whatever: I am happy; I am sad; I am angry; I am afraid. I am. Immediately after that rises, you are. What is it that creates this separation? This judging mind creates it. When we say let go of the mind, this is what we're speaking of. Let go of this judging mind. It tells you this is good; that is bad; I like this; I don't like that. This is pleasurable; that is painful. Give me more of this; give me less of that. I hope this lasts; I hope that ends quickly. Judging mind is what fragments the whole experience into pieces. Keep quiet. Don't let this judging mind fool you into thinking that this moment is not already perfect.

The minute you judge and say, "I don't like," it separates. Judgment goes very deep. It can go all the way into racial discrimination or religious discrimination, sexual discrimination or national discrimination, any kind of judgment that says you are separate. You are separate, so I won't share with you. You are separate so I will kill you if you cross my boundaries, if you try to take what is mine, or what is not yours. This judging mind not only creates the separation, but the wars that follow the separation. It creates a story about "others" and makes them the enemy. Jesus said, "Love your enemies." I say there are no enemies! They're just a figment of your imagination. Treat strangers as friends and friends as strangers. Treat allies as enemies and enemies as allies. It's all the same. It's only your mind that tells you, "This one's a friend; this one's an enemy. I can trust this one and I can't trust that one." Isn't this what happens? When judging mind rises, what happens? Trust flies out the window!

Whenever this judging mind rises, inquire and drop it. No matter what! Keep it if it feels good, and drop it if it feels bad? No! All the time. This is one of the beauties of impermanence: even this judging mind is impermanent. It passes. It's a passing thought, as long as you don't believe it. Let this judging mind come, and let it go. No one's saying don't judge. All the religions have said this for ages; what good did it do? "Thou shall not judge thy neighbor." Whether it's Muslims, Sikhs, Christians, or Jews, all the religions say don't judge your neighbor, but then they kill each other! This doesn't solve anything! Let the judgment come, but see it as judgment, or as I say, see it as B.S., a belief system. See it as that. See it as just judging mind, because it will pass in the next second. You'll ask yourself, "How could I have believed that concept so strongly? I was so attached to that point of view, and I see now it was just that, a point of view, completely meaningless in this moment." It was just a passing thought.

Trust is the key to oneness. Trust is the key to relaxing into the union that already is. That's all that stands in the way of enlightenment. This judging mind doesn't trust its own Self, doesn't trust this moment. So we can say to the judging mind when it rises, "Trust." Trust existence. Trust God, but instead of forcing yourself to trust, all you have to do is drop this judging mind. This is what surrender is, is it not? This sweet surrender that some of you have disappeared into? This sweet surrender saying, "I don't know." This is how you drop the judging mind: you inquire. Who judges? Who thinks he knows better? I do. Who is this I? And you look at it and you see, is this "I" real? Is this "I" who I am? At best, this "I" is my creation. It's the form that I created to play in this movie, to move around in this movie, but it's not who I am. It's a costume I'm wearing. You look directly at the "I.""Who am I?" And you let this "I" go. You drop this judging "I," no matter what and who you truly are reveals itself.

Consciousness is fluid and flowing; it's not static or stagnant. Let everything flow through you. Don't mind any of it. Then you see it was all just your creation, and you have tremendous tolerance for it. When there's no judging mind, you have tremendous tolerance, tremendous latitude for yourself. That creates space, and in this space there is grace. This grace is what allows you to wake up to the truth that you are already free; you are already One. In this space, there is no judging mind. You just love yourself; you love your creation; you love your movie. When you sit quietly enough, you see it's all you. It's all your movie. Love it. God loves it all. Be God and love it all.

Our lives are like movies. Get that. Your body, the circumstances of your life, your partner, your family, the people you work with, the people you drive on the highway with—it's all your creation. The whole world rises in you. Enjoy it! Don't take it so seriously! Then you can really appreciate it. The movie still plays out, but you become conscious that you're playing a part in this movie. As Shakespeare said, "All the world's a stage and we are merely players, strutting our hour upon the stage." Suddenly, money is Monopoly money. Suddenly your possessions are just props; your car is just on loan from the prop department. Suddenly your lover is somebody who was cast from central casting, your mother and father are actors playing roles, and you're playing out a script which you wrote a long, long time ago. You're simply replaying the same old scenario!

When you are identified with the character you are playing and you don't realize your life is a movie, and something goes differently than you planned, or a moment that you are attached to doesn't last, or a moment that you are repulsed by lasts longer than you would like, then you suffer. If you know it's a movie, you don't give a rat's ass, and you just live it! You live your life, knowing that it's a movie, and you let it play itself out. This is why everyone loves the movies, because you get to watch somebody else's life for two hours. You don't have to be involved in yours. Do that with your own life! Don't be involved. Enjoy it as a wonderful movie. Just remember you're not the movie and you're not the main character. This is just a part you're playing. For some of you, it's a comedy, and for some, it's a tragedy, or you can turn your tragedy into a comedy; it's up to you! Once you laugh at your life, you can never take it seriously again. Once you recognize the truth of who you are, you can never take the "I" seriously again.

The master actor, Jack Lemon, in speaking about the craft of acting, said, "If you lose your distance from the character, if you're too closely identified with the character, then it's a terrible performance. If you're too misidentified with the emotional roller coaster of the character, then it's a lousy performance. You must always have, in the back of your mind, the witness watching—knowing that it's just a play, knowing that you're just playing a part. Then the performance is informed by this wisdom, and you're not controlled by the part." He was speaking to all of us, the holy actors that we are, playing our roles in life. This is my invitation to you: play your role. Don't be afraid of it. It's the role you've created for yourself in this lifetime, enjoy it. Sometimes it's a tragedy, sometimes it's a comedy, sometimes it's a melodrama, and sometimes it's a soap opera—but enjoy it; it comes and goes.

You are the actor that stays aware in silence, watching a character in a movie as he passes through the screen of your Consciousness, moment by moment. When you blur it all together, it looks like it's a moving picture, but it's really one thought at a time. You think that it's a bunch of thoughts and you call it your mind, but really it's only one thought. This thought perceives itself as having a history, or a herstory. This is what they call in the movies "the back story." It doesn't exist. There is nothing behind that façade; it's just an illusion. There is simply pure Awareness. Even in those moments when you're involved in the play, it doesn't mean that you can't be aware that it's a movie. It just feels more real to you in that moment. You're playing the part more fully, but you always have to be aware that it's a part. Even when you get too involved in the movie, as long as you know that it's a movie, a role that you're playing, it doesn't matter. You know it's a movie, so those moments when it appears more real, celebrate them! Those are the heightened moments of your life. Then yell, "Cut! Print it," and move on to another scene.

Recognize the world as the movie that it is. See it as a movie and then act accordingly. Are you the character in the movie, or are you the one watching the movie? Sure, when you're watching a movie, you get involved for a moment, but you always know it's a movie. This dimension can be so much fun when you know you are God, the Creator, when you're not identified with your ego. Send the ego out for popcorn and enjoy the movie, because the ego is your servant! And while you're at it, drop the critic who's writing the good reviews and the bad reviews, and just sit and watch it. Imagine that someone let you into the movie for free; you didn't have to buy a ticket. You appreciate it more when you don't have to buy a ticket! You're here for free; you're here in this movie for free. So be free in this movie! Watch this movie without investment. If Al Pacino believed he was the intense part he's playing, or Meryl Streep the dramatic role, they wouldn't be able to go home and have a life. Although they must believe in the character, they also have to be aware of the camera and the lighting, but at the same time, pretend it's not there. Do you understand? This is acting. You know that you are making a movie, but you're pretending that you are not.

What is waking up? It's simply realizing the truth that you're playing a part in your own movie, that you're starring in your own dream. You begin to live consciously, what can be called lucid dreaming, where you know it's a dream. You know that if the police arrest you and you go to jail, this is only a part you're playing. You know that if you win the lottery, your character wins, but you, as the actor, don't get any richer because it's just a movie. You remain the same. So play your part totally, while being aware of what it is that motivates your character this lifetime. What's the theme? What's the desire or attachment that creates this misidentification with your character? That's really all you have to do. Investigate the "I." Look into its nature. You will see that it's just another role, another mask you're wearing to play the part in your movie.

You are dreaming, my love. This is all a movie! Wake up and realize that this is a movie and enjoy the show! Play your part; accept it. This is the key: accept your part, whatever comes. Just don't be identified with it. Wake up and enjoy your movie; play it out fully. If everybody plays their part, there is no problem, there is no suffering. Suffering comes from the misidentification with the movie, believing that it is real so you can't enjoy it. You get scared in the scary parts and upset in the dramatic parts, and you don't laugh at the funny parts! When you know it's a movie, you have a good time getting frightened and laughing your ass off at the ridiculousness of your character's point of view. My character has the funniest point of view, especially when he wants to be right! Or you find yourself arguing with your lover, and it's no different than being on a talk show, arguing a point. For what reason? You've been asked to be on this TV show; it's your life and you're the star. Enjoy it! Reinvent yourselves too; don't be afraid. Let each moment reveal itself. Improvise a little, ad lib.

No matter how turbulent your movie becomes—no matter how dramatic, no matter how horrific, no matter how humorous, no matter how intense the movie of your life becomes—don't forget that it is merely light and shadow projected on the blank screen that you are. When you disappear into Oneness, you realize that you are merely nothing, a blank screen, and all of the images of your life come and go. You remain blank underneath it all. This is the easiest way to live in the world awake. You know it's a movie, a lot of pictures on a screen, and you let yourself be blank, empty, and this Emptiness fills form. Sometimes the form is happy and sometimes the form is sad; sometimes the form is hungry and sometimes the form is full, but you are never the form. You are the blank screen on which the form is projected. Just remember this. In this Self-remembrance, a vast peace exists that can't be touched any more than the cinematic images can touch or damage the blank screen. No matter how many bullets Clint Eastwood shoots, it will not put a dent in the screen. No matter how many tanks pass by, no matter how many slashers attack, it will not tear the fabric of the screen in the movie theater. You are the blank screen. Let your movie play. Stop trying to control the movie and let it play out; this is my invitation to you. In this blankness, there is only bliss. Nothing can touch it. Nothing can take it away. Nothing can give it to you either. Be blank and watch what happens. Let yourself be surprised by the movie. You never know what is going to happen next.

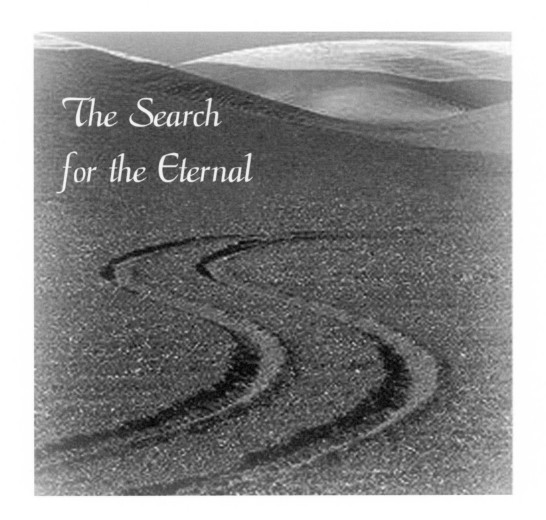

The Search
for the Eternal

To be reading this book, something must have motivated you. It may not be what you think it is, either. Something motivated me to go to India. I was searching for something, but whatever it was I was searching for, whatever name I gave it, there was no way I could know it before I experienced it directly. I could try to talk about it; I used to sit in the *chai tea* shops and discuss it. I could read about it; I could try to imagine it, but I could not know it. It could only be experienced directly, and it is through grace that I experience it now. In fact I am always experiencing it, because it's always now. Looking back, I realize what I was searching for all those lifetimes, and perhaps it is the same for you. It was the search for the eternal. Look and see. Have you not spent your whole life searching for that which does not change?

Whenever change happened, there was anxiety, there was fear, there was discomfort. As children, adolescents, as young adults, whenever you felt familiar with something there was safety, there was security. There was a sense of home, of belonging, and if that was taken away, there was insecurity. The search for the changeless is what has motivated your whole life. Look and see for yourself. You've been looking for eternal love. The whole idea that everything changes can be so unnerving that most people do whatever they can to deny it, to avoid it, to run from it, but the step to realizing the changeless is to totally accept that everything changes, the circumstances change, your point of view changes, your beliefs change, your emotions change, what's important changes. This is the truth. Everything changes. If you rely on any of those things that change, you will constantly be in turmoil and conflict with yourself. You will never be able to be at rest, at peace, because you're constantly trying to keep that which changes from changing. But if you surrender this need to control and allow the change to happen, you glimpse the changeless. If you accept what comes and goes as inevitable, if you really fall in alignment with this absolute truth, then it's easy to be at rest in that which does not change.

Your body goes through many changes between birth and death. If you're attached to the way it looked a few years ago, what do you feel? You can't rely on that which changes; you can only rely on that which is permanent. There's security only in abiding in that which doesn't change, so stop trying to impose the truth, the absolute truth, on the relative world. You can't stop your body from growing old, no matter how you try with human growth hormones, face-lifts, and fashions. You cannot stop the clock within the relative world. The body is born and the body dies; find that which doesn't die and abide here. Then you're at peace, no matter what happens to the form.

How much of your life has changed since you were born? These bodies have changed, the circumstances of your life have changed, for some of us our names have changed, but what remains the same regardless of change? It's so obvious that you miss it in your search for something other than what is. The circumstances have changed, the point of view has changed, the conditioning has changed, the opinions have changed; the flavors, the expression, the ideology, the religion, the likes and dislikes—they've all changed, but what has remained the same through it all? Look and see, for this is who you are: this constancy, this changeless Awareness. Realize this and all doubt disappears. All fear evaporates, for what is the biggest fear? The fear of death. When you realize the eternal, when you abide as That which is constant and doesn't end, what remains of the fear of the temporary? It becomes trivial, a moot point.

These bodies are constantly changing. They will change until one day they no longer breathe, for they are temporary. Realize this constant, unchanging Awareness, where permanence abides. Realize this permanence, and fearlessness is the result: implicit trust in That which you are, no doubt. Then the constant changing circumstances of your life, sometimes good, sometimes bad, are clearly seen as phenomena. It's so obvious that you can miss it, miss what already is, in search of what you imagine it to be. See the truth, that you were never born and you will never die, this Awareness that you are. Is it any different than the awareness that you had of your earliest memory as a child, as a teenager? Was this presence not there too? All of your memories throughout your life, were you not present for all of it? This constant presence is who you are.

That which doesn't change is formless; it cannot be known. It can only be directly experienced when you stop resisting the form that changes. Form changes; formlessness is eternal. Everything changes; nothing is eternal—but everything rises from nothing; therefore, everything is also eternal! This is what the Buddha meant in his Diamond Sutra: "Form is emptiness. Emptiness is form." The only thing that is constant is change. Form is constantly changing. Just an hour ago, a day ago, your point of view was so different than in this moment! Maybe some of you try to keep your point of view constant, like, "This is who I am; this is what I believe; this is the way life is." But this imposes a constant upon your point of view, instead of letting your point of view change organically. In one day I watch hundreds of points of view pass through my Consciousness, like innumerable characters playing Prasad, perceiving life through Prasad's eyes— and I identify with none of them. A whole host of perspectives are coming and going. Am I any of these?

Your point of view is here today and gone today, yet you hold onto it. If you surrender your point of view, what would you have left? If you let go of your problems, what preoccupation would you have to keep yourself busy? What would you do with all of your free time? Your mind is constantly changing. Whatever you think is gone the next moment. That's how meaningless it is, yet you give such relevance and such importance and such significance to your thoughts and emotions! They come up and they go out. If you really give permission to them, they are finished. If you give them significance, then you have to speak about them when they are gone. You have to analyze them, process them, keep going back and visiting them again. Let them be finished.

See how ephemeral your point of view is. It's constantly changing. It only appears to be the same because you're clinging to a particular point of view, one that you identify with. When life out there is somehow corresponding to your point of view in here, life is great. You feel good. But the next moment the point of view changes. Maybe in here or maybe out there. They become out of sync. What you're believing in here is not corresponding to what you're seeing out there. Why? Because the thought you're holding in here is not mirroring back in the way that you're used to or that you can identify with. It can't because it's constantly changing. It's just a lucky moment when the two correspond. I'm inviting you to surrender your point of view. Don't know who you are. Don't know where you're coming from; don't know where you're going to. Let go of the past; let go of the future. You are all longing to abide in this changelessness, in this constant Self that you are, this constant Awareness. Accept the change and focus on That which doesn't change. Not the body, not the mind, not the emotions—they change, but if you stumble upon that which is so familiar, and it's been with you always, and it doesn't go away, that's it!

The reason we seek That which is changeless, That which is constant, is because That is our true nature. The reason we avoid and run from that which is constantly changing is because it is ephemeral; it is impermanent; it is the illusion of appearance. It is the phenomena that appears and disappears on the screen of your Consciousness. Abide as That which is changeless and ignore that which changes. This is how you can discern between being awake and being caught up in the dream. Pay attention to the constant, That which is changeless, eternal, ever-present. Let go of your need for what is changing to remain the same. Accept change. Accept that which is changing and you realize the changeless.

top chasing that which is impermanent and realize that which is permanent. What is permanent is the ground from which what is impermanent rises. When you are abiding in what is permanent, everything is seen from this new frame of reference, the absolute truth. This is permanent, changeless. We start with no money and we end with no money—and the money comes and goes. The constant is having no money. The temporary state is having money. The mind wants to be secure by controlling that which is constantly changing, wanting more. It becomes a sickness. Who needs that much money? You can't take it with you. What about lovers? You're born without them, and die without them. The temporary state is having them. At night when you go to bed, you leave them. Do you dream together? Or do you dream by yourself? So when you go to sleep each night and surrender your body, where does your relationship go? Sometimes your partner may show up in your dreams, but sometimes it's someone else. What is the constant? What doesn't change when you drop your body and go to to sleep? What remains the same?

Whatever it is that you are participating in right now will end. Where does that leave you? Is your reaction, "What's the point? Why do anything?" Or is it, "I only have this moment, let me make the most of it?" If you really accept that you're just building a sandcastle and the tide is going to come in and destroy it, does that make any difference in the quality of your attention to the detail and the creativity of the sandcastle? If you know there is no future in the relationship that you're in right now, no guarantee that this person will stay any longer than this moment, does it keep you from loving totally? Does it keep you from giving your heart, being available? If you know that there are no guarantees that your work, your creativity, your expression will ever be seen or heard, or that you will ever be rewarded for your acts of kindness, does it stop you from doing them? Look and see. If you know it's going to end, does it change your participation in the moment? Or can you still be total? Can you still give it your all? If you have no guarantees and no rewards for your actions, can you still give it your all?

Know that life is a sandcastle. Know that it's impermanent. If you know it's impermanent, there's no suffering—because even when it goes, even when your tears are flowing, it's a good cry. There goes my sandcastle; I had so much fun building you! This is living in freedom: being available, seeing the world as your mirror and not being attached to anything, knowing in your heart of hearts that nothing really matters but playing as if everything counts. Then you realize what an adventure this life is! There isn't anyone left to suffer. It's just free-flowing Consciousness— constantly creating and responding to the moment, constantly available to love and share and dance in Emptiness.

In freedom, what is the point of working towards some future goal when there is only here and now? What is the point of going to school? What is the point of going to work? What is the point of planting a garden? What is the point of painting a picture? What is the point of making a movie? There is no point beyond the expression of this moment. You do it simply to do it, right now, to experience it totally with no attachment to the end result in the future. It is a total expression of the moment. Let go of all expectations of the future and free yourself from the rat race that keeps you running from death and pain, chasing eternal life and pleasure.

When you stop seeking, it doesn't mean that you just sit and do nothing—it means that even though you are not there to do anything, life still happens. How fantastic! The clouds still form, the rain still comes, the rivers still flow, the flowers still grow, and you dance amongst it all. You sing the praises of the Beloved in each and every moment. Every move becomes a dance, every sound becomes a song. This is God's paradise; this is who you are! We forget about it sometimes, when we're identified with this doer who has a goal, "One day I'll get that goal accomplished, and then I'll be in paradise." No, paradise is always right here, right now.

Who knows what the future will bring? Don't wait for it! Be available now. Wake up now to the truth that you are already free and you can be no other way. You are freedom itself! This is your nature. You are love. You are the love that you're seeking. You are peace. You are the peace that you have been missing. Look no further than right here. Whatever comes your way, no matter how horrible it may be—love it, be at peace with it, and set it free. Whatever comes your way, no matter how wonderful it may be—love it, be at peace with it, and set it free. Enjoy everything, but cling to nothing.

I'm here to tell all of you that you have an incurable disease. It's called life! What is born will die. Because your bodies were born, they will die. It's incurable, there's nothing that you can do—but if you accept it now, you'll be free. You'll be able to live out the rest of your days in freedom, and whatever happens to your body won't touch you. This is what it means to die consciously. It means the ego dies; the one who minds whether you live or die, dies. You're available to the moment, and when the body drops, it drops, just like a raindrop merging with the ocean. When you die, it means there's no more "I," that's all. When you die, the "I" is finished; the raindrop you have believed yourself to be is finished. The drop of water merges into the greater body of water and you become That. There is no longer any separation—it is all water and has always been water. What remains is the ocean that you truly are.

Have you completed with your life? Are you ready to let it go and be totally at peace? You don't know what will happen when you die, but who you truly are will remain. Only the body and the ego disappear. Who you are is permanent and cannot be destroyed. How can that be destroyed? Scientists say we cannot even destroy a particle of sand, no matter how hard we try; even if we blast the sand particle apart with an atomic bomb, it will not be destroyed. It will be broken into pieces, but it will not be destroyed. There is no device to destroy it; there is no one to create it. What we call creating is only rearranging things, and what we call destroying is only scattering here and there. The death that we're preparing for is the death of this "I." Look for truth and freedom only—the past is gone; don't romanticize.

Would you change your life if you had only six months to live? What would you do differently? Just look inside and see if there's anything in your life you'd be doing differently if you knew you had six months to live. What are you doing in your life that is no longer serving you, that is no longer your truth? What are you ready to let go of? What are your priorities? What are you doing in your life that is no longer relevant to who you are? It may be a job; it may be a relationship, or a responsibility you tell yourself you're supposed to have. It may be a story that you're still carrying. It may be something you're postponing, some unfulfilled desire. Give yourself total permission to be honest with yourself. What is yet to be finished in your life? What desires do you still harbor? What attachments do you still hold? Let them come up; let them go out.

You spend your whole life running from death, when all it takes is a second to change everything! That moment when the two cars collide, that moment when you go in for an ordinary checkup and the doctor finds a lump—this is part of life, admitting to yourselves that the death of the body can happen at any moment. You are not your body, and once you recognize this, there's only freedom. I have seen people wake up through their diagnosis of cancer or AIDS. It's just a device, an opportunity to see that you are not your body. Then the body plays itself out, the dream plays itself out and you have fun watching. You're not invested. If you're awake, you will embrace the moment of death. You will be available to it, to this wonderful transition, the dropping of the body. It is a moment of grace. There is nothing to fear.

Stop running and face the inevitable: this body will die because this body was born. That which is born will die—and will be born again, if you still have unfinished desires. You have had countless bodies over the centuries. Some of them have burned in fires, some of them have been shot, and some of them have exploded in war. Some of them have died of neglect and starvation, and some have simply died of old age. You've had so many bodies born and die, but how many times have you died consciously? How many times have you died the way the Buddha died? Have you ever let your ego die first, so that you could know eternal life?

Death of the body is easy; it happens by itself. Death of the ego is one of the greatest and rarest occurrences. Die consciously. Face it and be done with it forever. Free yourself now. Complete with the people in your life so that you can die free, and you don't have to come back next lifetime to do it. Do it this lifetime, so you can die in peace. We have this fear of dying our whole life, and then, when it comes down to it, when that moment nears, we make peace with it. Have you ever been with somebody who's ready to let go? It's like being with an enlightened master, someone who has made peace with the impermanence of this dream. That's basically what awakening is. So die before you die.

You will never die because you are not a thing. Only things like bodies and egos die, because every thing comes and goes. You are not a thing. You are nothing. You are not an object that you can perceive; you are the very subject. You are the constant that exists, no matter what objects of perception rise and fall in your Awareness. Stop being so busy with these objects that come and go. Let them go; let them come, let them go, and stay focused on that which doesn't come and go. You know it. You are it, and it's right here!

The flower's buds blossom, eventually withering and falling off the tree. The leaves turn yellow, and then they fall off the tree as well. The tree is bare, and then another season comes. When you are living in the root of who you are, none of those seasons coming and going bother you; they make no difference in your happiness. The tree doesn't mind when it drops its leaves, and the tree doesn't sing in happiness even when the blossoms come in the springtime. Its happiness doesn't depend on whether it's blossoming or shedding. Just recognize this: the root of who you are, the silence from which all of your creations rise, is untouched by the changing seasons. You are the unchanging Source, and everything else that changes is just a reflection of who you are. There are so many blossoms on the tree! The fruit is so ripe and ready to fall! Enjoy it. Play with it. Don't take it seriously. The fruit comes and goes, and it's delicious, but if you try to keep it, what happens to it? It gets rotten and stinky and smelly. Don't keep it, let it keep flowing, my love. Embrace the change that's happening in your life. Don't be afraid of it.

Nothing is permanent except for I Am. I Am the permanence that exists in the face of all impermanence. Whatever else comes and goes, whatever is impermanent, whatever relationships enter my life and leave my life, whatever jobs enter my life and leave my life, whatever family members enter my life and leave my life, whatever material possessions, whatever recognition, whatever it is that enters my life and leaves my life—I remain. This body enters my life and leaves my life, and I remain, for I Am the permanence of That. Realize That and no impermanence ever touches you again. This is your own Self speaking, saying I Am permanent; I have been here always, and I will be here always. There is no place I can go. I have come from no place and I will return to no place. I have been here forever, and I will be here forever. This is the truth! Nothing matters. There's only this bliss and this love and this compassionate overflow in every direction. The tree is in full flower! Smell the fragrance. It's intoxicating. Let yourself become drunk on this fragrance, the fragrance of your own Self.

Come out of the Closet as God

One of the greatest ways of escaping the realization that you are Consciousness is by putting realization in the future and seeking it in some practice. Another way to postpone it is to put it out there, on your guru, "He has it, and one day if I sit with him enough, I will get it too." Unless you walk into the room and see the one giving satsang as your own Self, you are doing nothing but setting yourself up for separation. Suddenly, you're the beggar, sitting at the feet of the king, hoping that maybe someday he will bestow his grace on you—and now you're in the future and you've missed. Recognize you're looking at your own Self. See that there is only one of us. There is only one Buddha, and there is only one Christ. You are the Buddha, you are the Christ, because who you are includes everyone and everything. This is a great secret that I am telling you.

There is nothing special about God-realization. The mind wants to make it special, wants to say, "This man is special. Let's worship him. He is the messiah; he will save us from our minds," but nobody gets saved, because they take his teachings and they make them into concepts to believe in, and then there is just more mind. Misidentification is what stands in the way of God-Realization, even if it is the misidentification of yourself as a disciple. Don't worship Christ; realize yourself as Christ! Don't worship the Buddha; realize yourself as the Buddha. Be yourself. Fall in love with the Self. We all have our own unique flavors, so don't try to be Jesus, don't try to be Buddha. Just be your Self, whoever that is. Give full permission to it, and remain as That.

For two millenniums, millions of people all across the world have celebrated Self-Realization through one form, which they called Jesus Christ. They have postponed their own awakenings while worshipping his. If you have been a disciple of any master through the years, you know this racket. It's called, "Let me worship you so I don't have to wake up." This postponement is based on fear. Waking up is not always comfortable. When you're free, sometimes you get crucified! What to do? When you're awake, you don't care! You're hanging on the cross; it's a little rough on the palms, but you don't care because you're not the form. Jesus didn't say, "Hey! Get me down; I've changed my mind." He didn't care in this moment. There was no attachment to form. You just play out the karma. But is it your karma to sit on the sidelines and worship somebody else and postpone your own realization? Inquire and see, who is this "I" who believes himself to be separate from Jesus Christ, and from all the other masters, and from everybody else? Who is this "I" who believes herself to be separate? Who is this "I" who believes? Inquire, "Who am I?" Look at the "I" and let it return from where it rose. See the source of this "I" and let it fall back into Emptiness.

Throughout the centuries, humankind has worshiped God outside of itself. This has been a total misunderstanding of God. Originally, this was designed as a device of humility to allow you to step outside of your mind, to stop identifying with your past and future, to detach from your conditioning and your expectations and to be still. In this stillness God is; this Awareness, this Existence that you are, is. It's been called God-Consciousness. It's the context in which your whole life happens. You are God itself. This is who you are, and the arrogance to think otherwise is what puts you in hell. When you are humble enough to admit that you are God and nobody else, you're absolutely nobody, then you live in heaven. Enlightenment is not the ecstasy or the bliss or even the open-hearted compassion that you feel. These are just symptoms. Enlightenment is realizing that you don't exist as an "I." You're not a separate "I." This "I" does not exist; you are That which the "I" arises from. When you drop this "I," it is Self-evident, always.

Let every day be Christmas, a Christ-birth day, and realize yourself in this moment. Don't make realization special: a Jesus or a Buddha every few hundred years. Everybody makes them special and wants to follow them. What is this need to follow? Instead of worshipping Jesus Christ, recognize the Christ that you are. Then you can really have a Merry Christmas! The tendency of the mind to look outside of itself—to make somebody else a saint and then to worship them—is so strong. The tendency of the mind to want to be taken care of, to be protected, to be rescued, and to feel safe is so strong. Our archetypal literature is full of these stories: the princess rescued by the prince, the superman who comes from another land, the messiah. Unless you realize yourself as the messiah, you are constantly afraid of losing the messiah. Instead of being a spiritually awake person, you become a religiously afraid person. You start to bargain with this messiah, with this saint or prophet or guru that you put outside yourself, and you behave in a certain way to gain the approval of this messiah. Then, like all messiahs, they become unavailable, and you have to start to please the ones around the messiah. They're telling you how to behave in order to get an appointment! Now it's political.

It's the nature of mind. You put something outside of yourself to pursue it, to attain it, to fear losing it, to cling to it, to become attached to it—and then you suffer because of that attachment, even if it's God that you are attached to. There's only suffering if you see God as outside yourself. As beautiful as the life of a devotee is, it's still not God-Realization. It can take away your suffering temporarily, just like when you fall in love. Suddenly, you're whistling. You don't mind if somebody cuts you off in traffic, but then a few weeks or months down the road, when the honeymoon is over, when the mind rises, when the challenges come, when the differences are seen, the suffering returns. It's the same thing with your spiritual awakening. You fall in love at first, but if you put the master outside yourself, if you put truth outside yourself, you will learn to hate it, to resent it, to fear it. That's why in this satsang we tell you right up front: you are That! You are the master; you are truth; there is no other. There's only one truth, and you are That! Absolutely, positively. If you're ready to hear this message, like the disciples around Jesus were ready to hear it, your life will be changed forever. The seed will fall on fertile soil, not on rocky ground where it won't grow. If you're fertile, the word of God, the absolute truth, can be realized in an instant.

See that you are the Christ-Consciousness you've been worshipping all along. You are the master whose feet you have been touching. It was simply a device to humble yourself enough to realize this truth. In this humility you realize: I am Consciousness; I am Christ; I am the Buddha. How can it be otherwise if it's all One? Every master who wakes up knows this: there's only one of us. There's no fighting amongst the masters. The fighting is amongst the minds of the followers who interpret the truth. Instead of looking at where Jesus was pointing, they got all busy looking at Jesus and then they fought about what he meant. Through the ages these conflicts became wars, and some of these wars are still raging today. This is the danger of worshipping the messiah outside of yourself. Don't put God outside of yourself. This is the mistake generations upon generations have made, turning God into an object to be worshiped on an altar. God is not an object; God is the subject. God is the One. You are this God, this Christ-Consciousness. This is the truth. Jesus said, "The truth shall set you free." Realize it, and it sets you free.

How do you realize God? If God is the seer, how do you see yourself? How can you see yourself? Have you ever tried to look at your own eyeballs? How can you see yourself? It's impossible. God cannot be seen, because God is the seer. In each moment, abide as the seer. Keep your attention on the One who is watching, not on what you're watching, even if it's the messiah, even if Jesus Christ himself shows up in some divine epiphany. Who cares? Who's creating this epiphany anyway? Who is creating this vision? Abide as the Source, because you are the Source. This source is Christ-Consciousness. It is your Consciousness.

Waking up is easy! Why is it that so few people up until now have allowed themselves to wake up? Ask yourselves, what stands in your way of simply waking up and realizing yourself as Christ-Consciousness? Is it because you still want to believe in this limited dream? What is it that keeps you misidentified with limited thought? Fear? Look for yourself. Be vigilant. Doubt? Unworthiness? "How could I possibly be Jesus? I'm not worthy"? Well, neither was he, but in that moment before death, in that moment when it was his darkest hour, he said, "Not my will, but thy will be done." This is the key. Can you be at peace no matter what happens in your mind, with your emotions, whatever happens to your body—can you just watch it all? Christ is nailed upon the cross, and he is watching it all happen. His last words are "Forgive them, Father, for they know not what they do." Wake up and be the light of the world. Shine the light on the darkness; don't be afraid. Tell the truth, no matter what, even if it means crucifixion.

You are born as Christ-Consciousness and you die as Christ-Consciousness, and in between it's all Christ-Consciousness. It can't be any other way, no matter what you believe. If you are going to believe in the Chosen One, choose yourself as that One! To realize yourself as Christ, you have to be willing to let go of whoever you think you are, because when you think you know who you are, you are stuck in misidentification. This is what stuck-ness is; it's arrogance. It's arrogant to think you know who you are. And what is arrogance but a defense against the unknown? It's just a defense. So watch this arrogant one, because he's the one who steals your freedom: "I'd rather know stuck-ness, which is familiar to me, than know freedom, which is unfamiliar to me." If you're willing to really humble yourself and say, "I don't know anything; I don't know who I am," then who you are is revealed in the unknown.

Realize beyond a shadow of a doubt that you are God, that you are the creator. Then recognize the beauty of your creation, however it shows up! But don't get identified with your creation, with these lives you lead, these bodies you live in. Don't be identified with your art. Identify only with the artist. The paintings, they come and go; the books, they come and go; the movies, they come and go; but the artist is constant. You are the creator of your life. You are already God, and you have been misidentifying with God's creation when you are actually the creator itself. Just realize this simple truth.

Instead of perceiving yourself as somebody who is praying to God for a better life, see yourself as God who has created a body to explore life, like an innocent baby. Babies don't have minds. They don't have to pray to God, because they don't feel separate from God. What is God but Oneness? What is mind but separation? The baby doesn't perceive itself as separate, not until the ego develops when she is around two years old. Until then, a baby lives in complete trust and is taken care of, and if she is not taken care of, she dies. She can't even fight to survive. She can't manipulate; she can't resist; she can't do anything. She is helpless. The ego is based on this first experience of being helpless. All of your ego's fears originate from this initial memory, for what would happen to a little baby if she were abandoned or rejected by her parents? She would die. This is the source of all your fears of rejection and abandonment. See through it. Let the past go and begin anew. There is nothing to be afraid of. It's all in your mind.

J esus said, "Come to me as little children." This is what I say to you. Free your mind. Face your fears. Be helpless. Trust Existence. Trust God. Be open and vulnerable, like a new-born baby. Don't know who you are. Let each moment reveal itself without expectation or plans, or if you make plans, have no attachment to their outcome. Expectation leads to suffering. Simply set aside your beliefs, your fears and judgments. Set aside all of your conditioning through religion, culture, and society; all of it, all of your identifications with yourself, whomever you believe yourself to be. Just set it aside, right now. Don't know who you are.

on't postpone another second. You are free! You are God! Now act like it! Be God. Be free. Celebrate your creation. Don't be like a painter who can never finish his painting: just a little more here, a little more there. Then it's a painting that's never finished. No, finish your painting. Finish this moment. Be your masterpiece in this moment! Recognize that there's only one creator. You are That. Rest in That. No doubt. There's no authority greater than your own, and I'm not speaking about mind or doubt or judgment. I'm speaking about That which exists as the Source of all mind, doubt, and judgment. There's no greater authority than your own. You are the great authority; you are the creator. Stop doubting it and take full responsibility! Stop playing the victim; stop being the judge; stop trying to improve your life and just be. You are the Master and you are Peace itself. You are the Master Peace.

Drop all doubt. Ultimately, the removal of doubt is all that it takes to realize truth, to finally accept that I am already That which I seek, and to stop searching some place else for this realization. It's right here and now and has always been here and now. In truth, you're not being asked to do anything; in fact, you've been asked to undo everything by doing nothing. The removal of doubt happens in an instant, when you're doing nothing, and in that stillness you have a direct experience of your true Self. This is how your doubt is removed, through this direct realization, in this silence. There is one moment when your mind drops, and what remains is That. All doubt disappears, all fear disappears, all projection into the future disappears, all regret disappears. You—as you have known yourself to be, as a conditioned ego—disappear. What remains is what some call God.

What is more important than abidance as God? What can possibly be more important than to abide as the creator—some creation? No. How can it be? How can the creation be more important than the creator? The creation is temporary; it comes and it goes. The creator is permanent; the creation is impermanent, so don't pay attention to the creation. You have wonderful creations, coming and going in every moment. Don't pay attention to them. Abide in the silence. This is where the creator abides. When you are identified with the creator, with the unmanifest, the unknown, the mystery, then the known comes and goes. Once it's known, its days are numbered. It has risen and it will fall; all great empires rise and all great empires fall. All wonderful relationships begin and all wonderful relationships end. A baby is born and an old person dies. This is the nature of duality. Don't waste your time on that which dies. Focus on that which is eternal. Focus on God.

It is time to come out of the closet as God and accept this creation that you've allowed to come through you. Celebrate it, nurture it, take care of it. Stop running from it, stop judging it, stop trying to make it something other than what it is, so that it can fit some expectation from the past. It's time to wake up and see the perfection of your own creation! This is what happens when you drop concept, when you drop pursuing, and when you drop the need to achieve anything. In silence, the perfection of who you are is directly realized. Let it be so.

It's your destiny to be free. It is your destiny to be awake, and nothing you do can stop this. Nothing you do can make it happen either; you might as well face it. You're awake! You're awake, you're free, and let's be done with it. How can it be this simple? This is what the mind always says, it can't be this easy—but yes, it is. It has to be easy. If it's not easy, then it's not it! It's easy because it's your natural state; it's easy because it's who you are, before you add all the complications and complex concepts and ideas. It's easy to be free. It takes a lot more energy to be ignorant—you have to believe in a lot of things— but if you believe in nothing, it's easy!

Look and see what complex postponements and concepts you tell yourself, that keep you from reveling in the magnificence that you are. What story can you possibly tell yourself to postpone freedom, to postpone joy and love? Is it that "I'm a miserable, good-for-nothing, worthless piece of ego"? You think, "This ego will never be good enough; how could I be God when I'm just this lowly ego? I can pray to God, love God, be devoted to God, but how can I be God?" Jesus said, "You cannot be a servant of two masters." Make your choice: God, ego; ego, God. It's up to you. The beauty of it is, when you choose God, it also includes ego—but when you choose ego, ego doesn't realize it's God. Ocean, wave; wave, ocean. The ocean knows it's all of the waves, but the wave does not know it's the ocean.

There was a time when beings such as ourselves would have to spend days and weeks, months and years in rigorous settings, in difficult sadhanas, practicing, practicing, to realize Self. What I say to you is, it's your destiny to be Self! You can't be otherwise, whether you realize it or not. It is your destiny to be Consciousness, so there is no more need to postpone that realization. We are moving out of this period that they call in India the *Kali Yuga*, the age of darkness, of ignorance. Consciousness is freeing itself from its illusion. The veil is dropping. The dreamer is awakening from the dream and realizing its true nature. You are all a reflection of That. Unquestionably! This why we gather in satsang, for the simple recognition of who we are: Consciousness Itself. It's an effortless, easy recognition. All the other lifetimes of rigorous practice have prepared you for this moment right now. Your merits have brought you here right now. The longing, the yearning to remember Self, has brought you to this moment right now! It's time to graduate. Nothing more can be done.

Wherever Consciousness places its focus, wherever you place your focus, you become that. If Consciousness places its focus on this body, on this form, it is easy to believe that you are this body, this form. If Consciousness focuses itself on fear, it is easy to believe that the world is a scary place. If Consciousness focuses itself on desire, and success, it's easy to believe that life is either wonderful or terrible, depending upon what level of success is happening that day, and which goals are obtained. But if Consciousness focuses on nothing other than the Subject, not on any object, Consciousness itself is revealed. It's as simple as that.

You have to work really hard to stay miserable. You have to work really hard to keep this identity going. Haven't you ever noticed, "It's such hard work being me?" Have you ever heard yourself say, "It's so hard to walk in my shoes?" Take them off, walk barefoot and drop this "me." This is the invitation to freedom—be finished with this struggle and this strife and this misidentification. Just relax and be who you are, whoever that is! Have no idea who you are. Have no idea what's right and wrong. Have no idea where your life is supposed to go. Have no idea what enlightenment is. Then you're empty; then you're available. You know that whatever rises is just your mind. Some kind of challenge arises, great! It's another opportunity to drop misidentification, to drop attachment—to be free.

Don't know who you are. Be available. Let Existence live you each and every moment. Be unknown but aware, so that you can live your life and not be touched by the personality and its story. Keep quiet in the storm, be still in the turbulence, so that you can be empty when there's a lot going on around you. It will not disturb your peace because there will be nobody to be disturbed, just a lot of emotion and a lot of motion; it's not who you are. I see you all as free, because you're my own Self. You are free. You are Existence. Don't believe your story that tells you otherwise.

What is it that your heart is longing for? Maybe your heart is longing for nothing—then you are very lucky because that is what you are here to get this lifetime: nothing. If you can get hip to that, you will be free. The truth is, you have come with nothing and you will leave with nothing. What to do? If you think you come here with something, call it karma; or to get something, call it desire; or to leave with something, call it attachment; then you are in big trouble! Then there is only suffering. If you recognize you have come with nothing and you leave with nothing, and in between there is just a lot of nothing—then you can have fun! Then you see there is nothing to do, no one to be, and you are simply available. This is the secret to happiness!

This realization of nothing is available to everyone—Not by anyone, but by no one. It's not something you understand with your mind, not something you even feel with your emotions. It's a non-knowing. It's a non-doing. It's so deep; it's at the root of your being-ness. All you have to do is drop deep, deep down into the root of this being-ness, into the silence of your own heart, to experience this nothingness. Believe in nothing. Rest in nothing. Celebrate nothing, and then you're always celebrating!

This truth is available for everyone because truth belongs to no one. Once you recognize it, it's easier and easier to keep quiet, not to mind your mind, not to perceive yourself as separate, not to see yourself as owning anything or identifying with anyone. Simply be still and watch it all come and go; sit by the ocean and watch the waves rise and fall, ebb and flow. Stop struggling in the surf. Come and sit on the bank and watch yourself rise and fall and ebb and flow. Stop drowning in your mind. Come as you are; be still and watch. Be still, and the ocean of your own Self drowns you in ecstasy. Don't look outside yourself; watch yourself. You have all of the answers, and they are available here and now. Your own life holds the key to unlock this imagined prison. Don't look outside yourself for the answers.

Find out how you sell yourself short. Is it a past story about having a wounded heart, your lover leaving you, not making enough money? Or is it a future story about how others like Buddha, Jesus, and Ramana Maharshi get enlightened, but not you, not yet? Enlightenment does not happen in the past or future. It only happens now. It's only happening now. What stories do you tell yourself that prevent you from realizing your enlightenment? You are awake, my love. Whether you believe it or not, you are awake; you are God-Consciousness. I know this because I am That. I am Aware. You are Aware. There is only this Awareness—No guru, no disciple, just awake beings sitting together in silence.

Don't be shy; don't be complacent. Expose your Self. All you have to do is drop this one thought, this "I" thought, whoever it is you believe yourself to be; it always yields who you are. It's a moment by moment Awareness that I am nobody. Nothing is happening; whatever I think is a lie, any of my opinions are just that—opinions. They are meaningless! My life is meaningless. My identity is completely meaningless. Where I'm going, where I've come from has absolutely no relevancy to truth. You just recognize this and celebrate it. This is what it means to be nobody in a world full of some-bodies. You just accept that you're nobody—and there's such freedom in this acceptance! It's your destiny to be nobody, and as nobody it's your destiny to be the Prince of Peace, the Son of Man, God of Gods, and Lord of Lords. This truth is considered blasphemy. A few centuries ago, I would have been burned at the stake for speaking this way, but I am simply the messenger. You are the One. It's your destiny.

Embrace your awakening; each one is unique. What do you think? You have to go to the desert and spend forty days and forty nights, like Jesus? You want to go sit under the bodhi tree for seven years like the Buddha? Embrace your path; embrace your life. It's not a path to go somewhere, it's just your life as it's showing up this time. You created it. This is your mystery; you're unlocking the treasures through your own unique issues, stories, and identifications. These all hold the key to free you. All you have to do is accept them and then drop them and say, "I am not my story; I am not my identity. I am no label, I am no body, I am no one."

Thoughts rise and fall, sensations come and go, emotions rise and fall away. Simply be aware now of who is aware of all of this coming and going. Who is aware? Who is watching the rising and the falling? In stillness, you can watch: when you move toward the thought, you engage in the thought; when you resist the thought, you're engaged in the thought. In stillness, you can watch it rise and fall. No engagement, no identification. This is why I invite you to be still, to keep quiet. You watch each thought come and go, especially the thought that begins with "I." In this stillness you see the identity rise and fall; you see your tendencies come and go, you see your story appear and disappear; you see the issues of your life come up and then fall away. There's no identification with them; they don't touch you. This is what happens in stillness.

Many of you have meditated for years. Now, instead of simply watching the thoughts and watching the sensations, watch the watcher. Turn your attention on attention itself. Abide as pure Awareness, and whoever you have believed yourself to be appears and disappears as a thought. This "I" is never to be believed in again when you rest in the silent Awareness of your own Self. It doesn't mean the "I" won't rise, but it won't be believed; it will simply be seen. If you see the "I," you are not engaged in "I." Keep still. The past rises and falls; the future comes and goes. You are not identified with any of it; you are That which does not come and go. You are stillness itself. Rest here. Don't let the past hold you back; don't let the future distract you. Rest here and now. This "I" is nothing but past. The minute "I" rises, it's past. It's past identification. It's past conditioning. It's past story. It's past attachments. This "I" that rises—it's future. It's future desires, future stories, future expectations. This is all that mind is. See it and be free.

Who you are is ever-present, just pure Awareness. Pure Awareness, watching the "I" rise and watching the "I" fall, watching the story come and watching the story go. None of it touches you; there is no one to suffer. Awareness does not suffer. God does not suffer. When thousands of people die in a hurricane or a flood or an earthquake, God does not suffer. God is simply the Awareness in which all of these tragedies rise and fall. Only mind suffers, because mind says it should be different. I want what I want. Make life meet my expectations. I should be different; this form should be different. This is suffering, and it's all based on past. Let it go. Be still. It rises and falls—don't pick it up. Be still. No matter how real it appears, it is not real; it's your mind telling you that it's real. Don't mind your mind. Be still.

D on't be fooled by your I-thought that thinks it knows who it is. It is simply a thought, vying for your attention, "Look at me, look at me. Aren't I special? Aren't I important? Aren't I unworthy? Aren't I in trouble? Aren't I good? Aren't I bad?" This is what the I-thought is all about: give me attention, like a needy child pulling at your apron. This "me" is never happy. You can never please it. See this "me" for what it is. Ignore it, and it goes away by itself. It goes away by itself if you don't touch it. In Consciousness, all kinds of fragmented thoughts and concepts rise and fall, pleading for your attention like an orphanage full of children. "I need help. I'm afraid. Feed me. Take care of me. Gimme, gimme, gimme." These are your thoughts, your orphan thoughts. When you adopt them, when you identify with them, then they feel at home. They feel good, but you become burdened. The lightness of being, this freedom, this enlightenment that you've tasted gets bogged down, becomes heavy, and you feel like you've lost it. This is because you're too busy trying to take care of whatever your mind is minding in that moment. Don't be fooled by your mind.

Whenever mind rises, inquire, "Who cares? Who cares when the mind rises?" Only mind. "Who cares when there's fear?" Only mind. "Who cares when there's desire and aversion?" Only mind. Don't mind the mind and you can abide in this freedom forever. Existence is offering you so many gifts! Take what is being offered. The mind desires what it doesn't have, and doesn't want what it has, what is available. This is the nature of mind. This alone is reason enough to drop your mind. It's crazy! Absolutely crazy.

B e still. Let your personality come and go, just like the clothes you wear. Your personality can change just like your costumes do, because you remember that it's just another costume. In freedom, any personality is used in the moment by Existence, the Existence that you are. Keep still, and simply watch Existence create the moment. Don't chase whatever impulse your mind tells you to: that desire, that fear, that attachment. Simply keep still and watch. Let it be fresh and new. Have no idea what you're going to say, no idea where you're going to go, no idea where you've come from. Simply be in the freshness of the moment, the innocence of That creating itself in unlimited vastness, creating itself in freedom. This is what's available if you don't mind your mind, if you don't rely on the past as a guide for how to live your present, if you don't spend your present looking around the corner at your future. Just let yourself be.

Be open and available and watch what happens. This is all you have to do—be available and watch. Concepts rise and fall throughout the day and throughout the night while you're sleeping. Keep still. Don't follow them anywhere. Let them come and let them go. This is freedom. You can be free while your mind rises. You can be free while you have a host of emotions playing like music on the radio, different melodies throughout the day: blues, country, rock and roll, and jazz. You have full capacity to press the button and change the station at any point. But why, when you can just let the song play out? Another song will come on soon. That's what emotions are for, to be enjoyed. It's part of being alive.

One of Papaji's greatest messages was simply to do nothing. It's one of the greatest challenges that we as Westerners meet: to be willing to do nothing. People get confused as to what that means. They think they have to lie around like couch potatoes, doing nothing! This is not the essence of what it means to do nothing. What it truly means is that you surrender any personal sense of doer-ship. You surrender the "I" who thinks he's doing something. Whether it's something great or something horrendous, it is only the mind; it is only the mistaken identification with mind that believes itself to be doing something.

Look at your life and ask yourself, "How much of my life am I doing and how much is simply happening?" The truth is that you are not doing any of it. It is all simply happening, but the mind loves to take credit for it. The mind loves to get the attention; that's what it thrives on. It pats itself on the back or judges itself as horrible, depending on its particular story. It's the same "I," the personal "I," the doer. The American culture is based on the pioneer, and this individual sense of doer-ship created what is called "freedom" in America. Free to be an individual, not to be controlled by a government or a religion or the powers that be. The whole culture is based on a sense of rebellion and individual doer-ship. Since this is what is defined as freedom, it can be very difficult for an American to recognize what true freedom is.

True freedom is freedom from that sense of individual doer-ship. It's a recognition that this individual "I" that I believe myself to be, as separate, as willful, as shameful, does not exist except as a concept. Look and see for yourself. The individual doer, the individual ego, the individual identity that you believe in has changed through childhood, adolescence, and adulthood. It's constantly changing because it's simply the form. Freedom is recognizing that this constantly changing form is not who you are. It's simply a shell, a costume. This individual "I" is only a mask you put on to meet the moment. It's a product of your conditioning, your American culture, your Judeo-Christian religion, or whatever your culture or religion may be. It is a result of your identification as a man or a woman, black or white, gay or straight—whatever label you identify with. In freedom, all labels are dropped. In freedom, you surrender your identity, the misidentification with an individual "I," and realize the unchanging, formless Self that you are.

The individual "I" can be very tenacious, so what motivates it to let go? Some are motivated because the suffering is too intense. Others have had the good grace to have this "I" disappear in a moment of silence and have recognized the truth of who they are. The individual "I" disappears and merges back to the Source from where it rose, and in that moment, it is undeniable who you are. Then you can put the costume back on or not, you can let the "I" rise or not, but there can't be the same identification with this "I" any longer. It's seen through, it's exposed. That's when surrender follows: the surrendering of this personal doer-ship, the surrendering of any sense of will power or even personal choice. The "I" can choose, but does it really have a choice? It's choosing from such a limited palette; it's choosing either fight or flight. It's choosing to do the same old song and dance, over and over again in the name of individual freedom, in the name of autonomy, in the name of rebellion, but it's still running from the very thing that it's identified with. Stop running. Be still.

Recognize that this personal "I" is nothing but a thought. See the "I" rise from Emptiness and return to Emptiness. There is no personal doer. There is nobody doing anything. So if we are not doing anything, who is? We drive our car and we end up in satsang. Who is doing it? If you are not this me, this ego, this individual personality, who are you? Drop the misidentification with the doer and find out. Let go of this "I" just for a second and do nothing. If you do not identify with the doer and simply be still and do nothing, then it's easy to recognize who is doing it, who is guiding the circumstances of your life. It takes tremendous trust to discover this truth and to let go of this misidentification with doer-ship. This is called surrender.

The mind makes up a big story about what surrender is, "Do I have to surrender to someone, to a guru?" First, ask yourself, "Am I living in surrender?" If the answer is "no," inquire, "Who is this I?" And let the "I" return to the emptiness from which it rose. True surrender is recognizing that this "I," who thinks he or she is in charge, does not even exist! Surrender is inquiry. It's the same. When you inquire you see that the nature of this "I," who thinks he is creating the moment, making the choices, doing the doing, does not even exist except as a concept! When you can see the truth about this false "I," then surrender has already happened. The one who's afraid of surrendering doesn't even exist. There is nobody to surrender. It's like when you're in a car and you're about four years old. Your Dad is driving next to you, and you've got one of those pretend steering wheels, and you think you're driving the car. Take your hands off the steering wheel for one moment! Do nothing for one second, and discover the Source of who's doing everything.

This "I" who thinks he or she is in charge is deluded. It's delusional to think that this "I," this limited form, is creating your life. This is arrogance! This is why on traditional spiritual paths you have to lay your head down at the feet of the master and get it chopped off! This is the arrogance that Jesus referred to when he said, "It's easier for a camel to pass through the eye of a needle than for a rich man to enter the kingdom of heaven." How do you free yourself from this arrogance? Through surrender. Not my will but thy will be done. The "me" who thinks he is in charge disappears, and God's will is seen as the driving force, the creative force of your life. In the moment, when there is no "I," you see that there is no separation between you and your life, between you and this moment, between you and the awareness of this moment. There is nobody in the way trying to be in charge, trying to be in control.

Ask yourself, "What is it that keeps me identified, that doesn't allow me to simply let go and trust and enjoy the ride?" This is all that has to be surrendered, this misidentification with the "I" who needs to control, this doer. See through it. Surrender this misidentification through inquiry. Ask yourself, "Who brought me here? The body? The mind? Who is doing my life? Who has created my life?" Recognize the mystery! "God has created my life; God is doing it all. I think that I'm driving the car, but it's really on a track—so I let go and let it take me." You simply watch your life unfold. You don't see where this vehicle is taking you, where the tracks are leading. Who knows; who cares? You stop needing to be in charge. Not *my* will but *thy* will be done. Suddenly, the "I" realizes it's not in control, that God is running the show, that God is the Source of this life, and it's ready to surrender control. And who is it surrendering it to? Some God up in the sky? Some guru sitting in front of you? Some higher power? In inquiry, you see that this "I" doesn't exist, and therefore was never in control to begin with. You let it go, and it falls back to Emptiness. In that Emptiness, all that remains is God—and you realize God as your own Self. It happens instantaneously.

Life is happening by itself right now. Your heart is beating, your lungs are breathing, your hair is growing, and your cells are replicating. Life is happening by itself; you don't have to control it. Drop this "I" who's identified, who's afraid, who thinks he or she is in control. Drop this doer who's trying to do everything right; trying to do his job right, trying to do her relationship right, trying to do satsang right. Then you'll see that your life is guided by Existence. While you're breaking free of the doer, it can be a little scary. This is why I'm here, to hold your hand. Do you trust? That's all you need.

Can you trust, unconditionally, that whatever is, is? It doesn't matter what you think about it, what you care about it, or how you feel about it; it just simply is. If you can trust that implicitly and explicitly, then you're free. In that moment, there's no mind; there's no doer. There's simply the quality of is-ness, of Existence. In that moment, there is no separation between you and what is; you are merged with Existence. It's all happening by itself; you don't have to do anything to make it happen: it's already happening, has always been happening, and will continue to happen. Drop the doer and do nothing. Just be still and watch. You are not separate from anything. Everything you see is you; it all rises in you, from you, and as you. It only appears to be separate—the way one hand appears to be separate from the other hand, like branches on a tree. Follow them down to the source. Follow the branches down to the source, to the trunk of who you are, and you see that it's all One.

The moment you surrender, your life is no longer your own. In fact, you realize it never was. It belongs to Existence, to God, to your true Self. The "I" gets out of the way effortlessly. It no longer is trying to do its life. It no longer is searching for success, for attention, for approval. It no longer takes credit for anything and no longer is blamed for anything either. It's no longer in suffering and no longer in pleasure. Nothing matters, absolutely nothing. There's nobody who cares, and Existence lives your life. It's Existence's life to begin with. Who said it was yours?

The Silence of your
own Heart

Those of you who have realized truth, you are the prophets. Go into the world and share the truth; share it in a way that is unique to you, in your own flavor. Tell the truth, what you have realized—that you are freedom, you are love, and you live in heaven, which is here and now. You are heaven itself. You are living in heaven and heaven is living in you, because heaven is here and now. So now what to do? The true sage would say, "Nothing!" If you are truly out of the way, then there is nobody in the way to do something or to do nothing, and Existence simply happens. It happens through you and as you, in you and outside of you and all around you. All you have to do is give yourself permission to trust Existence; to trust the grace that you are.

The kingdom of heaven is at hand! The kingdom of heaven is here now! There's nothing you have to do to earn it; there's nothing you can do to earn it. It's right here now. It's always here—but give yourself a path to follow, a stairway to heaven, and you put yourself in hell. It may be limbo if you're lucky, limbo or hell, but it's not heaven. Don't put heaven at the end of a path. Don't make it a goal. Don't make it some place you are going to in the future. It takes tremendous devotion to truth to bust this illusion of heaven in the future. It takes extreme commitment to freedom to bust this delusion that you're not already free. All the religions talk about renunciation, but in truth all you have to renounce is the "I" who believes she's not free. The "I" who thinks he has to do something to attain it. The "I" who's more interested in the process than the truth. The "I" who's more interested in getting there than simply being here. Finish with this search, renounce this belief, and then you'll see you're already in heaven. You don't even have to desire heaven; simply accept hell and it becomes heaven!

Give yourself permission to be God incarnate, to be love in form, to be the Buddha in your daily life, to be both the master and the disciple. Give yourself permission to be That which you've been seeking your whole life, and let it express itself. This is the invitation. When you stop being a seeker, and you become a finder, what can you do but share it? You can't hoard it; you don't hoard the truth. When you wake up, you can't contain it! You can't keep it in! You give it away. You throw it away. You're giving it away constantly. When you give satsang, it's because you can't hold it in any longer, and truth speaks through you. But beware, you might get into trouble. You might lose some friends. You might get fired from your job. So what! Jesus got nailed to a cross! How much is heaven worth to you?

Be finished. Stop looking outside yourself; be finished. Be finished with gurus, be finished with pursuit, be finished with religion. Start your own religion right now in this moment, by just being free. People will start to follow you around, and when they do, tell them, "Go, just be free. Don't follow me around. Be free just like me. I am your own Self." Tell them, "There are no two; there is no difference between you and me. There is only one of us, and this One has realized freedom. This One is free." That's the truth. This One is free, so be the One, realize yourself as One, not as two, not as me and you. This is separation. Whether you do it with your lover, whom you're desiring from, or you do it with your enemy, whom you're fighting with, or you do it with your guru, whom you're worshipping, whoever you do it with, stop and realize the truth. There is no one outside of you. There is only One Self, and you are That!

All your practices are postponements, because the practice presupposes that you're not already Free and you have to do something to become Free someday in the future. All of your pursuits, all of your hopes and desires and wishes and insights and revelations and epiphanies and relationships and endeavors and good works and kindness and sharing and caring, it is all meaningless. It comes and goes. In freedom, it's simply a flat line of silence. Sometimes the line curves up like a smile, and sometimes it curves down like a frown, but there is nobody to call it happiness or sadness.

When you are ready to drop all identification, whatever it may be, as a healer, as a teacher, as somebody who needs to be healed or somebody who needs to be taught, when you are ready to finish, this is silence. Silence isn't just sitting in meditation; silence isn't just not speaking. Silence is when you are no longer identified with "I." You have no worries, no fears, no stories; they come and go, but they don't touch you. You know you are That. You know you are the Source from which this whole dream rises, and there's no fear, no doubt, because you know it's a dream. You know it's not outside of you. How can you fear that which you are? No beginning, no end, no body. You rest in this truth: you are That; you are free. You are the Buddha. You are freedom itself!

We come to satsang not to learn anything, not to get anything, but to sit in freedom. Just be free without conditions, without concepts, without ideas, without goals, without futures, without pasts, without relationships, without possessions, including this body that comes and goes. Bodies come and go, stories come and go, but you are free. Freedom is permanent; freedom is constant. This is who you are: constant, eternal, unchanging, unwavering. The rest comes and goes. It is temporary; it is not who you are. Do not mind it. Do not listen to that which comes and goes; do not believe it for a second. You are free. It cannot be any clearer than this. No searching, no doing, no identification, just the silence of freedom.

Welcome to this silence that you are. It's never-ending silence, constant, never-changing silence. No matter how noisy your mind may be or may get, the silence always remains. It's always available to fall back into. It's the Source of who you are. There's no need to worry if your mind gets a little noisy once in a while. No need to fear. All you have to do is inquire. Who's making all that racket? Who cares? Who's worried? The answer inevitably arises, "I am." Now let this "I" fall back into the silence from where it rose, and you effortlessly abide in silence. The noise is a symptom of this "I." Remove the "I" and you remove the noise, then there's only silence.

Trust the silence of your own heart over the noise of your mind. Whenever somebody who's making noise rises, whenever something takes you out of the silence of your own Self, inquire. The greatest gift you can give to yourself is to inquire. This silence is ever-present. It's who you are, regardless of how noisy your mind may be. You can always rely on the silence. It is the background against which all of the notes rise and fall in the melody of your life. The sound always rises from silence and returns to silence. This is the nature of music. Music would not exist without silence, and these lives that you're creating would not exist without silence either. Realize the silence that you are as the background against which your lives happen. Realize this as the context in which your life rises and falls. Realize the Source in silence, and then whatever story you have is completely seen as noise. Once you've recognized the silence, anything that happens in your life is clutter, dissonance, ramblings of the past; it's clanking and clanging, but it's not silence. Abide as the silence. You are this silence.

When you close your eyes, everything disappears and there is only silence. Thoughts rise from this silence and fall back into silence. This is why Papaji's only teaching was, "Keep quiet." This doesn't mean to take a vow of silence and not speak, like people who go on long retreats. They sit in meditation for ten, twenty, thirty days in silence, and then they come out of meditation and their minds are chattering again. This is not silence! Silence is your natural state; it's the Source of who you are. It exists even while speaking. As noisy as it may seem sometimes, the silence is ever-present. It does not come and go; it's the constant. Find the constant silence, which does not come and go, and rest here. All suffering comes from relying on what is impermanent and depending on that which comes and goes. Discover That which is constant, this ever-present silence, and you're free. The mind gets noisy, and it does not touch the silence. The personality comes and goes, and it does not touch the silence, for you are silence itself.

It's a mystery how you can just sit in satsang and recognize the silence. You can feel it, this presence. If you're open, if you're available, the mystery that brought you here is revealed to you as your own Self. Then the chatter of your mind can be stopped. The suffering can end. Realization is possible here and now: the realization of this silence, this love, this ever-present presence. It's a mystery how some of us recognize this while others continue to suffer. It's a mystery why we were misidentified for all of those years, all of those lifetimes, and can drop this misidentification now. Realize this silence. Let the misidentification with personality just return back to the silence, to the mystery, to the unknown.

To not know anything about yourself—this is what it means to be in silence. In silence, you don't know who you are. Somebody asks, "Who are you?" and you can't say. You remain quiet, and your presence speaks for itself. The presence is the absence of "I," of mind, of noise, of ideas and concepts of the known. You surrender to the unknown. It takes tremendous humility and courage to surrender to the unknown. The noisy mind wants to know; that's what keeps it activated—running towards what it knows to be good and running away from what it knows to be bad; seeking what it knows to be pleasurable and avoiding what it knows to be uncomfortable or painful. This is what keeps the "I," the mind, active. In silence, there is no seeking and there is no avoiding, there is no running to and there is no running from. There is simply stillness. You keep still and you let the thoughts rise and fall. They rise from silence and they return to silence. You keep still and sit in silence, in love, in truth.

Fall in love with silence so much that even the sound of your own mind is too much for you. The chatter of your stream of consciousness, your ongoing editorial, your play-by-play account of your life is too noisy. You fall so much in love with silence that when your story rises it's too cacophonous; it's too disharmonious; it disturbs your peace, and you stop believing your own thoughts. You learn to be so quiet that your own essence reveals itself before story, and sustains itself during story. You are now no longer interested in your story: you see it rise; you see it fall; and it doesn't interest you anymore. This is how you're not distracted by your mind. This is how you don't engage in your thoughts. This is how you keep silent.

Abide in silence by not being interested in anything that rises in your mind, no matter how horrible, no matter how wonderful. You have to be done with all of it. Finished. It doesn't mean your life won't still continue, but you will not be engaged in it; you will be abiding in silence. You will be totally attentive to nothing. When you are totally attentive to nothing, then Awareness is free to realize itself as Awareness. When you engage in something—whatever concept, whatever idea, whatever story—Awareness believes itself to be that. Engage in nothing, abide in silence, and then no thought can catch you. Then you are abiding in pure Awareness. You see your story rise and you don't pick it up, and then you see your story float away. It doesn't touch you. It may be a physical story; it may be an emotional story; it may be history or herstory, but it doesn't touch you because you are abiding in silence. You are no longer interested in the noise, no matter how exciting it may have appeared in the past.

The silence is sublime, and it is who you are, unknowable, unspeakable. It's the mystery of your own Self, where anything is possible. Silence is the abidance in this non-identification with anything. Things are like musical notes, rising and falling as melody. The silence is the background. This is who you are; you are the silence. You are not the notes, as beautiful as they may be; you are not the notes, you are the silence. You are the silence from which the musical score of your life rises and falls. The notes rise from silence and return to silence. Don't get caught up in the melody. Abide as the silence and the music is delightful! Whether it's dramatic, whether it's staccato, whether it's melodious, whether it's harmonious, it doesn't matter. You have complete tolerance for any kind of music: hip hop, country and western, disco, rock 'n roll, or classical. It doesn't matter because you're abiding in the silence from which all music rises and falls.

If you have a life where you can sit at home and meditate all day long, then sit still and meditate. No problem, close your eyes and meditate. If you can live your life this way all day, that's beautiful. But for the rest of you who have to go to work every day, take care of the kids, drive in traffic, deal with taxes, navigate your relationships—for the rest of you, you can be vigilant in your day-to-day awareness. This is a practical freedom that doesn't go away just because the mind rises. Use the circumstances of your life to free yourself. If something rises don't be afraid of it. If you can drop it—beautiful. If it drops by itself—even better! But when you're engaged, be honest with yourself. Inquire at that moment, "Who am I?" and follow the I-thought back to the source. Whatever it was that was engaging you will fall away effortlessly.

Use all of your focus and all of your energy to wake up to the truth of who you are. Stop trying to save the world and realize that the whole world, and your body that travels through this world, is all part of a dream that travels through your Consciousness. Awaken to this truth, and it will rock your world! Even though the world will appear the same, it will be intrinsically different. Even though you will still go to work, and be in a relationship, and participate with your family, and chop wood and carry water, the truth will change everything—not only how you relate to yourself, but also how open and trusting you are in the world, because now there's no fear. How can there be fear? Fear is only a result of the misidentification with separation. When that is dropped there's no more fear, and you realize that you are the world, you are the light of the world.

Whatever thoughts rise, pay no attention to them; keep quiet. Whenever the I-thought rises, see it clearly; look at it directly. Is there identification there? Do you believe yourself to be this "I" in this moment? If so, inquire, "Who is this 'I'?" Follow it back to the source from where it rose. Look to the source; from where does this world rise? Where does this "I" that you believe yourself to be rise from? Look. Find the source of your being. Find the ground of your being and abide here. Don't be distracted by the objects of your mind, the objects of your desires, the circumstances of your life. Who cares? It's just mind. It's the present comparing itself to the long gone past and measuring itself against an unseen future. It doesn't exist; all that exists is the Awareness in this moment. You are this Awareness, so be aware. Beware of the mind; be Awareness itself. Keep this single-pointed attention, stay aware of Awareness and don't let your mind be distracted.

Whatever thought rises in your consciousness, if you engage in it you will believe yourself to be that thought, you will limit yourself by that misidentification, by that label, by that form. A man, a woman, American, European, Indian, Christian, Hindu, Jew, Muslim, gay, straight, whatever the label may be, you will limit yourself through any identification with form, with thought. Angry, sad, afraid, guilty, unworthy—any thought, whatever it is, if you engage when it rises in your consciousness, if you believe it, in that moment you will feel as if you are that. Stay quiet no matter what rises; don't point the finger outside yourself. Watch your own mind so that you're not identified with it. Watch it. Look at the source from where this mind rises and keep quiet. This is called vigilance. This is how you can sustain the freedom, the bliss, the peace that you feel in satsang in your everyday life. Every time this "I" rises, you don't indulge it. This is mind. Drop it. Then expression and communication and feelings all happen by themselves. When there's nobody who needs to be heard, then God speaks, the God that you are.

We come to satsang for to see through the "I," to see the "I" as ephemeral and as impermanent, as simply a thought arising in the Consciousness that we are. If your "I" thinks he got it, if your "I" thinks she knows, if your "I" thinks that what he or she is doing is important, meaningful, relevant—then this "I" is being kept alive and identified with. Satsang then becomes just another concept for this "I" to take on and hide behind. It learns the lingo and it shows up, does the right steps. It basically creates a new ego, so that it won't be found out, so that it won't be seen as the truth of what it is, non-existent. Become vigilant to truth, and simply see that whenever the "I" rises it is completely meaningless. Even when it says "I got it," even when it says "I know," even when it says "I'm awake," it is still meaningless. It is still just an "I," it is still just a concept, and now this "I" has taken freedom—which is no thing, which is silence itself, which cannot be known—and conceptualized it. "I'm no one, I live in nothingness, I'm the silence, I'm free." Unless you see through to the nature of this nonexistent "I" as a concept, as a mental construct, you will stay misidentified.

What takes you out of freedom? What allows you, as Consciousness, to engage in thoughts and believe them as real? What story do you tell yourself to postpone the full realization that's available here and now? What keeps you from seeing the truth, that mind comes and goes but you always remain, desires come and go but freedom always remains? To answer these questions you must get quiet enough, get still enough, to watch the nature of your mind. Just watch it. Nothing to do but observe. Your mind thinks you have to do something, but freedom happens by itself. The very doing, the very trying to get free makes you feel less free, more engaged. It's like a car that's stuck in the sand and the tires are spinning and spinning; the more it spins, the deeper it goes. So stop! Do nothing. Keep still. Be aware, watch, and all the tendencies of the mind will rise. Don't believe them; don't resist them; don't engage in them. Just watch. Don't even have a watcher who watches. You are the pure witnessing that's watching it all come and go. Freedom doesn't happen from a third-party witness. This is a misunderstanding of meditation, this third-party witness who believes, "I'm watching now, okay, I'm watching this and that." No, this witness is mind, and it goes, too. It falls away in silence. All that remains is pure Consciousness.

You are pure Consciousness. As long as you keep your attention focused on it, the tendencies of the mind play themselves out and are finished. Whenever they rise again there are no roots; they are seen as thought and no longer believed in. They have been exposed for the lie of the mind that they are. Whether it's shame, unworthiness, fear, doubt, or judgment, "That's just my story; that's just my personality type, that's not who I am." When these tendencies rise, it appears that the joy and the love and the presence of God are not available in that moment. That's only because the personality identification obscures it like the clouds in front of the sun. The sun is always shining, no matter if it's cloudy or if it's nighttime. The sun is always shining!

Love is like the sun; it's shining all the time. Your mind, like the clouds, obscures it. You need to have your sight to see the sun. This is why you come to satsang, to get your sight back, not just to glimpse the sun. You want to see the truth of who you are as love; this is why you're here. Only the mind, this blind "I" who's terrified of love, who's so scared of love, who's so scared of being annihilated in love—is standing in the way. If the "I" offends thee, cast it out! Cast out this "I" who's afraid of love and fall in love, right now. Don't postpone a second longer! Don't hold back a second longer. Fall in love; don't be shy. You are love itself! Focus on love, love loving love, and mind doesn't have a chance. It melts like a snowball in hell because mind is frozen; mind is dead; mind is stuck. Love is fiery; love is alive; love is passionate. So the mind, when it's faced with love, when it's surrounded by love, melts into a puddle of nothingness.

Anything that happens in your life that crystallizes this "I," that makes this "I" seem real, seem important, or creates a defense and a need to control or judge—drop it. Be discriminating and drop it. Choose a life that allows you to be quiet. If you are constantly distracted by your mind, drop that which distracts. If the "I" rises and gets caught, no problem. Let go again by inquiring, "Who's caught? I am. Well, who is this "I?" And let it fall back into the true Self that you are. Let the wave fall back into the ocean. Remember, even when the wave rises you're still the ocean. Even when a thought is identified with, you're still absolute Consciousness. This is the best news of all! No matter what you believe, no matter what you think, you're already That: Freedom, Love, God Consciousness. Drop the "I" and you can experience it directly. Now you can start fresh from this moment. You are born again.

There's a treasure buried in your backyard, and you're counting pennies in your kitchen! Look deep within and you will see this treasure. It's always been here. It's not something that you achieve through any effort; you just recognize it. Stop identifying with anyone or anything. Renounce your past and be here now. Have no future; just be available to this moment. And when mind rises, and chances are it will, don't mind it. For those of you who are awakening, let your mind alone. You don't have to control it; it comes and it goes. Emotional reactions come and go, don't waste your energy trying to control them. Use all of your energy to keep quiet. Just because your mind rises is no indication that you are not already free. Do you expect in freedom that you will not have a body? You have a body and you have a mind, so what? Just don't identify with them. Don't care; don't engage. Let it come and let it go, don't resist it and don't believe in it.

Don't get caught up in the imagination of your mind. This is what robs you of your peace, like a thief in the night. Make nothing important, only nothing. Once you do, then you are available to everything. When you realize you are nobody, you can be anybody. You have no idea or expectation of who you have to be or what is supposed to happen, but you are completely open and available to what needs to happen in the perfection of the moment. You realize yourself as pure Awareness with nothing obstructing it, no idea, no belief system. This is God: pure Awareness. You can abide here. You can abide here and still take care of business. You can abide here and still have fun! There is no more separation between what is work and what is play. There is just this moment of pure Awareness, the silence of your own heart

Living in Freedom

You are already free. You can't do anything about that. Whether you see it or not, whether you recognize it or not is irrelevant, because either way you are free. It's your nature. There's nothing you can do about it! If you don't see that you are already free, it's because there is someone who is attached to some past idea of yourself or a concept of what freedom is. Drop this and you will see what I see when I look at you. You will see yourself as free. This is because there is only one of us, and this One has always been free and will always be free. So drop your searching, drop your doubting, drop your judging, drop all the belief systems and be free. Then watch how freedom manifests in your life in its own unique flavor. This is the joy of waking up! We are each a different flavor of ice cream, and you can be your own unique flavor. This is the beauty of awakening today. We don't need another Buddha. Somebody please tell the Buddhists! They are all imitating him; they all want to be vanilla ice cream. We don't need another Jesus. Please, somebody tell the Christians! We've had plenty of chocolate. Create your new flavor of ice cream. Let the world taste you for the first time in freedom. Be free; this is your nature. Enjoy it; be delicious!

L iving in freedom is so unique to each of you that it's easy to miss it. The realization is universal, but the way the realization reveals itself is unique. It's as unique as your ego, as unique as your fingerprint, and if you try to do it the way that somebody else did it, it's just your ego trying. It's as if we're all sitting in school and we're painting pictures. Are you going to look over your shoulder and paint yours like the one next to you, or are you going to let this painting rise from within you and express itself in its own unique way? This is how you live in freedom.

When there is no mind, in satsang, in meditation, during those few seconds of orgasm, it's easy to be free. Honoring the moment as it presents itself, seeing it as completely divine and perfect, and not minding the mind when it rises and falls—that's the challenge in freedom. So, let go. Drop all concepts of who you are, what freedom is, what it's supposed to look like, and how it's supposed to happen. Recognize that you don't know a damn thing about anything! This is how you keep quiet in your daily life. Don't mind your mind when it rises. Don't pay attention to the old patterns as they play themselves out, and don't care anymore about anything. Then let your Self express itself—full-tilt boogie, moment by moment, however it does. There's nobody left to mind.

Freedom is like walking on a tightrope with no net, no net to catch you. It's dangerous, it's alive, and it's free! It's not safe, and it has nothing to do with feeling comfortable or feeling good or getting your desires met or being taken care of. It has nothing to do with any of this. It has to do with when you no longer are identified with a separate "I." You are finished with this "I." Then you've realized yourself as Existence. No matter what you're doing, there's never a doubt. Existence is doing it; Existence is speaking through you. Existence is moving you in the dance called "life." There's never a doubt, there's never a fear, for how can you fear your own Self? There's only fearlessness in freedom.

Every move you make is perfect; every word you speak is perfect. There's no doubt; it's pure love. You never have to go into your mind and think ever again, "Should I or shouldn't I? He loves me; he loves me not." You don't have to think; you are free to be. You never have to look outside of yourself for any authority. In this moment of freedom, your guru is dead. The guru has been realized as your own Self and the form is finished. There's no more need to honor some religious figure, be it Jesus, Buddha, Papaji, or Osho. It's finished in realization, because the realization is that there's only One. You realize that you are Jesus, Buddha, Papaji, and Osho. How can it be otherwise? There is only One.

When you wake up and see that you're already free, you realize that you have always been free, and that whomever you have believed yourself to be as not free must have been a lie. When you're willing to come to satsang, open your mind and your heart and say, "Yes, this is my truth, too. I'm free; I've always been free," then all of your effort to realize yourself, all of your practice, all of your karma is seen as a lie. You can be attached to it, or you can see through it and see that it is a lie. Not only is the past not happening now, but it only happened in your mind! So, where is the karma in this? Karma is the tendency of the mind to repeat itself, over and over again. If you don't believe this mind, if you finally realize that I am not who I thought I was, then there is only freedom. Does freedom have karma? You have realized God. Does God have karma? When you realize yourself as God, whatever false identity you were that had karma falls away, and when it rises, again you laugh. You see the tendency rise; you see the pattern rise; you see the issue come around again to be looked at, and you laugh. You can laugh; it's just a story! It has nothing to do with who you are.

Freedom is not what you think; it never is. It's a moment-by-moment Awareness. The minute you have a technique or a method, you're dead. But if there truly is no way, then how do you discern, in your daily life, between what is serving you in your freedom and what is not? When you let go of this mind that knows what is good and bad, how do you discern? How do you get out of the way enough to let life happen? It's easy to talk about it in satsang, but how do you live it in your daily life, in your relationships, in your jobs, and with your children? If there's no mind to decide, who decides? Who discerns? Does anything go? You've heard me say, "Everything is perfect," and this is the truth on the absolute level, but does that mean you're not accountable for your actions? Does that mean it doesn't matter that children are slaughtered, that husbands kill wives, that there's greed and corruption and pollution? Does it really mean it doesn't matter? On the absolute level, it definitely does not matter, because this is all a dream, but do you just walk around saying, "This is all just a dream; it doesn't matter?" Of course not. That's why I always say nothing matters, but everything counts. On the absolute level, nothing matters, but in the relative world, everything counts equally. So live like every moment counts.

Waking up is just the first step. How one lives in freedom in the world, one could call this mastery. How do you allow the circumstances of your life to fall into place in a way that serves Self, that serves God? How do you allow all of your senses to be there to support the experience of God-Consciousness instead of the ego with its tired, old fears and desires? How do you discern what is God's will, and what is your ego's will? All of the rules are thrown out; there's nobody and no conditioning to base it on. There's no scripture. How do you live your life in freedom? How do you know whether to come to satsang or not? How do you know whether to stay with your boyfriend or your girlfriend? How do you know whether to go to work? How do you know what is right and what is wrong? You only have to ask yourself one question, "Am I serving Self, or am I self-serving?" If you are self-serving, you are on your own, in the same pattern you've always been in: looking for love in all the wrong places, being disappointed, suffering. But if you offer yourself, your whole life to serving Self, then Self takes over. Then everything happens in grace. Nothing is up to you. Whether your relationship is working, whether your relationship is ending, whether your relationship is beginning, this is all up to Self. Whether your body is healthy, whether your body is dying, whether your body is being reborn, this is all up to Self. Your only job is to get out of the way and serve Self, until you have realized yourself as this Self.

Offer up your egos. Offer up your needs. Offer up your desires. Offer up your fears at the feet of Self. Give them up. The world is filled with people on their own, and they're fighting and hurting each other so badly! They don't know how to share; they don't know how to care for each other, because they believe they are on their own. When you surrender and serve Self, there's only one Self then. It doesn't mean you have to deny your own self. It means you're allowing Self to take charge of your life instead of your mind, with all of its conditioning, all of its beliefs, all of its limitations. You're serving Self, and then Self returns the gesture and serves your mind. Self serves it in every way. It may not be what your mind wants, but it's exactly what it needs.

When you stop seeking a goal called "enlightenment," or "happiness," and you realize it as your natural state, what is there left to do? First, you fall in love with truth. This is *bhakti yoga*. Then you inquire and you see the one who fell in love with truth doesn't even exist. This is *jnana yoga*. Then you are in surrender, and you spend the rest of your life in *karma yoga*, in service. What else is there to do? When you have realized that there is no "I" and there is only one Self, what else is there to do with your incarnation but be available to serve? If you think your life is about making yourself happy, then you'll never truly be happy. If you think your life is about getting something, then you'll never get it. You'll never get what it is you're searching for. Give it up! Make yourself available and Self will use you. It's a great job and the benefits are fantastic! You can continue your life, chopping wood and carrying water: driving to work, going to the office, teaching school, playing music, painting houses, supervising factories, giving sessions, teaching dance. Whatever you're doing, you can continue doing it all while serving Self.

Every moment serve Self, serve God. Then you're working for God. God is the boss; ego is the servant. Set your egos straight! You're working for God! Let them know right off the bat. The mansion belongs to God. Your egos think that they are the owners of the mansion because God is out of town. God is not around. Take back the mansion from these egos. It's the butler pretending to be the homeowner. It's the maid pretending to be the matron. Put them in their rightful place. Let them serve God instead of serving their own selfish needs. Ask yourself, "Is this for my ego or is this for God?" Discern in your life like this. Live for God. Keep the ego focused on God whenever the ego rises. Be vigilant and watch it. Make it so that everything it does, it does for God. It's no longer in service to its own selfish desires and aversions. This is called surrender. When you live like this, your life is no longer your own. The ego is in surrender to God, and then it's effortless to live in freedom and serve God.

Once you've realized yourself, the natural inclination to serve is self-evident—it happens by itself. You just give, organically. What else can you do? If there is an itch you scratch it. You don't say, "Let's negotiate which hand will scratch it first; I scratched it last time, you scratch it this time." It happens organically. When you see that everything is a reflection of your own Self, of course you're there to serve. You don't have to be trained. The churches and the religions with there commandments that impose these rules on you create nothing but resistance. Anybody who is told what to do is being ripped off, robbed of that graceful experience of moving into compassion. Compassion is not something that can be imposed on you. It organically results from blossoming in freedom.

When you are no longer trying to wake up, when you're not trying to feel better, your mind is quiet. You're living in love, giving and receiving love in every moment. Give yourself what you've been seeking for lifetimes. Find out the truth of who you are! Finish with your questions, with your search, with your doubt, with your misidentification, with the idea that you are doing anything. Stop trying to do your life, and let your life do you. Make yourself available for life to express itself through you, for life to live you. You don't have to struggle anymore; you don't have to search anymore; you don't have to practice to achieve anything anymore. Now what is there to do? Nothing. That's the answer. Well, try doing nothing for the rest of your life! Try doing nothing and see what happens. It's quite impossible to do nothing, but you can be available to let God do you, let Existence do you. This is what we call *non-doing*. Do you see the difference between doing nothing and non-doing? When I say, "Do nothing," it means that you don't take any credit or blame. Whatever happens through you is Existence. Existence happens through you, around you, in you, outside of you, as you.

There may still be challenges in your life that prohibit you from flowing as fully and totally as you can, where the river of Existence is dammed through decisions that you've made, or belief systems that you still hold as truth. They're just rocks in the river, and when too many of them gather, one on top of the other, it creates a dam. But the river is stronger than the rocks—the river passes over the rocks when there's enough river. Free yourself from the misidentification with these rocks and be the river of life. No matter how tragic, traumatic, or significant the story may be from your past, you have the opportunity to see it as a rock and let it sink into nothingness. Let your river run free, and let the rapids approach! This is exciting; this is juicy! Most people are ready to turn back when the whitewater rapids show up. Those of you who are courageous enough to go through it, I'm right here with you! If you find yourself going over the waterfall, this is where we meet in truth, in the absolute truth that nothing is real. When you let yourself realize this, you go over the falls without a barrel, and you disappear into the ocean.

One of the dangers for those who are awakening is a concept of enlightenment as being magical and mystical. That's why masters like Sai Baba who perform magic are so popular in India; everybody loves to see magic. Now you see it, now you don't! In freedom, when you wake up, you realize how magical this moment really is, how miraculous this breath is and how utterly amazing this life is. In this light you can see how totally ordinary magic is. Magic is when the mind experiences something that it cannot explain. In truth, it's completely ordinary for those who can see beyond the mind's explanations. When I was in India, I saw a statue of the elephant God Ganesha drink milk right out of my spoon. At the time, all of the statues throughout India were performing the same miracle. It was amazing. It was mind-blowing! For what is a miracle? A miracle is beyond mind. So drop your mind and you will realize the miracle is your own Self. Abide as no-mind, and watch the tendency of your mind to seek magic.

Nothing changes when you realize yourself. If you're waiting for your problems to go away, for your soul mate to appear, for the winning lottery ticket, then you're deluding yourself. Drop this concept that your life is supposed to work! Your world does not necessarily change when you realize yourself, but your perception of it is completely altered. You still may have problems, but you don't consider them to be problems anymore. You still may have debts, but they're no longer burdens. You still may have relationships, but you are no longer dependent on them. You still have a body, but you're no longer attached to what it looks like and how it functions and how long it lasts and what it feels like. You are free.

We can play together as waves, dancing with each other, smashing into each other, immersing each other, realizing that we are the ocean and these forms are nothing but waves. Then life takes on a whole other quality! You take full responsibility for your experience, knowing that you have allowed this wave to rise, and you can surf it or sink into it at any moment. You don't have to finish riding the wave all the way to the shore. You can just ride it for a few minutes and see what it feels like—and then drop it, drop into it. You don't have to finish anything as long as you are finished. You can walk away from any relationship at any moment; you can walk away from any task. You don't have to do anything because you see through it all, but if the impulse rises, you can participate in anything because you have no fear. Let go and see where the river takes you. Celebrate the whitewater rapids. Let them finish you. So what if you get thrashed around a bit! This is how the rocks get smooth. Just let go. Let the river carry you back to the ocean of your own Self.

Fall in love with your Self in the perfection of this moment. Want nothing more than this moment, nothing more. Have no expectations in the moment; simply be available to this mystery called you, for you are the mystery. Don't know who you are; don't try to understand who you are. Don't limit the mystery that you are, this vastness, this pure I Am-ness; don't limit it in some misidentification with a thought. Let it go. Don't grasp it; don't engage it; let it go. The thought may be anger; the thought may be depression; the thought may be lust; the thought may be greed, envy, jealousy—it doesn't matter. It could be the most enlightened thought that you could possibly have: "I know the meaning of life!" Let it go. Don't hold on to your highest epiphany; don't hold on to that moment of enlightenment, whatever it was, because that moment is in time. It's now dead. Enlightenment is here now, always. It's here and now, beyond time. You can't know freedom; you can't know God. You can only love God. Ego can just love God. Let yourself love freedom so much that freedom is all the ego thinks about! It only wants truth. It's ravenous for it, and it gets swallowed up by its own appetite! It loves truth so much that it is consumed by it. This is what it takes.

In satsang you catch fire with truth. It overpowers you! Any mind has no place. Any history or her-story has no place. No past, no future; endless, and timeless. You don't have to do japa or yoga, meditation or chanting, studying or learning. You don't have to do anything to attain what is unattainable, for if you attain it, you can lose it. What is possible is a direct realization here and now. It's only here and now! Let go of your expectations, let go of your ideas, let go of your concepts; just let go of whatever it is you believe in this moment and keep still. In this stillness you reveal your Self to yourself, and once you get it, it's got you! It's unexplainable, this truth, but once your heart catches fire with this truth, there's nothing left to do. You're at its mercy; you're at the mercy of truth. It's got you! All you can do is surrender.

Satsang is not like going to church or temple. You don't come once a week and feel good about yourself, and then go out into the world and feel guilty because you are not practicing what you learned. You don't come to worship anyone; you don't come here to get anything. You come here to drop everything, and in this dropping, the truth of who you are is realized effortlessly. Satsang is where we gather to recognize the truth of who we are in a way that is so undeniable that it transforms us forever. It really only takes one moment for this transformation to happen. If you are lucky enough to fall in love with satsang, you will realize this intuitively. You will know it to be true because it is your own truth. This is the absolute truth. There is only one of us, and this one is pure Consciousness.

You come to satsang; you fall in love with truth, and then your life shows up a certain way and your mind tells you it should be otherwise. Your mind tells you, "I should be beyond that," when it's your very mind that's creating it to begin with! This is the time not to mind your mind. Just let it be; don't touch it, don't pick it up, and then it will drop on its own. It comes and it goes. These thoughts are absolutely meaningless, and so are these emotions that we're feeling, but they're an expression of the humanness we're playing. How wonderful! When you're no longer identified with form, no longer a prisoner of duality, then the pain is as exquisite as the pleasure. It's the same. The sadness is as eloquent as the joy. It's the same. There's nobody who thinks one is better than the other, nobody who is resisting the dark and seeking the light. This is all seen as mind. You're simply being aware and allowing whatever comes and goes to come and go. Then it plays itself out; then you're finished. You let yourself finish. You get out of your own way and let your life finish by itself.

Something incarnated you. Something created this dream. Some thought, some desire: finish it! Don't get in its way, don't repress it, let it finish itself. You can drop it, yes, how beautiful! Drop it if you can; if you can't, let it play itself out. It cannot faze you anymore than a wave can faze the ocean. It's just a wave, rising: of anger, or sadness or lust or despair. It's just a wave in the ocean that you are. It rises and it falls by itself when you abide as no thing. These things don't touch you. There's nothing to be afraid of. You don't have to resist them; you don't have to do anything with them; you don't have to work on them. It'll work itself out. It's like a storm; the waves overflow and then they come to silence themselves. The storm comes to calmness; the swell returns to stillness; it always does by itself. Trust That.

Do you still think that you know what you need to be happy? "If I only had that thing, then I'd be happy. If I only had a little more money, if I only found my special lover, if I only had a better place to live, if I only had a healthy body, if I only get enlightened—then I'd be happy." Do you still think this? Give it up! Give it up now. See that this is a trick of the mind, and it will take you from paradise in an instant. What is it you desire? What is it you spend your days doing? Trying to make your life fit some expectation or idea in your head of what it's supposed to be? It never turns out that way, anyway. Why waste that effort? Let it be. Let it be what it is. Stop efforting. Stop trying. Use that energy to be aware of what is, and watch the miracle of your life unfold.

Why spend so much effort making plans that never work out the way you really want them to? It always shows up differently in the moment; it never shows up the way that you plan it. How can it? Maybe if you're really good at manifesting, maybe if you put in a lot of energy, years and years, lifetimes of effort, you finally get the payoff. The business makes the money; you land the lover; you have the success you're looking for. Years and years you put into one moment! And then, "Oops! I got it! Now what?" Some people spend a whole year planning for Christmas! Why plan? Don't waste your energy in that direction. Use your energy to be aware, and in this Awareness it's easy to see that this moment is perfect. When the one who is planning is out of the way, it seems all the more perfect, because it's showing up however it's showing up. Not according to your idea, not according to your expectation, but just the way it is.

The realization of the truth of who you are allows you to constantly let go of whatever rises and allows it to fall back into Emptiness by itself. Resting in this silent Awareness, you watch yourself appear and disappear, your life rise and fall, the circumstances come into existence and then not exist any longer. This is freedom. It's not a concept. It's not something you pursue. What I'm speaking of cannot be achieved—it's your natural being-ness. It happens when you stop pursuing, when you stop trying to achieve, and when you drop all concepts. The realization is instantaneous, here, now. The way to effortlessly abide in it is to continue to drop whatever rises. Then it's easy to keep quiet.

In freedom your mind will rise—years of conditioning, how can it not rise? But you can simply inquire when it rises, "Who cares?" When you let go of this "I" who cares, it's easy to embrace the moment as perfect. "Who cares if my best friend won't speak to me anymore? Who cares that my husband's walking out on me after twenty years of marriage? Who cares that I can't afford to buy a new car?" You see, any of these conditions on your happiness prohibit your happiness. Have no condition and see the perfection of the moment. And then, like true Zen, what you desire could happen anyway. Your friend comes back to you; your husband suddenly doesn't want to leave you; the money comes when you let go of the need for it. It's a funny game Existence plays with itself: whenever you're not looking for it, it comes. This is why we tell you to stop looking. Stop looking for freedom, stop seeking and it will find you. You see? It will find you.

If your mind did not rise, you would not be in this world right now. Without thought this world would not exist. For better or for worse, it would not exist, and this body would not exist either, for this body rises from thought as well. We free ourselves from the misidentification with body-mind by returning to the Source from where thought rises, by abiding before mind, prior to thought. When you abide in the silence prior to thought, you're able to recognize mind and not believe it, not engage in it. Then mind comes and goes, like day and night. It comes and goes, like your breath. You inhale and you exhale, a thought rises and a thought falls—there's nobody to engage, just pure Awareness, pure God-Consciousness. This is who you are. You are beyond mind. You exist before thought and after thought. Don't postpone another minute; recognize this truth.

Are you willing to try living life alive and in the moment, just watching what happens, no expectations, no plans, no ideas—just letting life reveal itself in the moment? This is freedom. Freedom is not some high state of Consciousness that is only attainable by the few. This is not liberation; this is a concept! Liberation is liberation from the mind; that's all. It's when there's no one thinking, when there's no one minding what is. When there is no mind planning, controlling, resisting, judging, criticizing, rebelling—or at the very least when there's no one identified with that mind when it rises. It can rise, but you, as Consciousness, do not have to engage in it. Be vigilant. Watch that mind, as Ramana Maharshi would say, like you're watching a tiger in your room, a tiger that is ready to pounce! That's how vigilant you have to be. If not, it will bite you; it'll eat you, and you'll find yourself inside the tiger's tummy.

When the going gets rough, don't let your ego go into defense. Say "yes," embrace whatever the challenge is. Keep quiet and watch. When the heat gets turned up and the burning becomes so intense you can't stand it one second longer, go beyond that—and in that moment you've gone beyond the "I"—beyond the "I" who likes and doesn't like, beyond the "I" who wants and doesn't want, beyond the "I" who fears and doesn't fear, the "I" who's caught in duality. These moments are your wake-up calls: when you're standing there, watching your son take his last breath from terminal illness; when you're watching your lover walk out the door; when you're watching your business go bankrupt; when you're watching your own body get old and die. These are the moments when the veil is ripped open and you see beyond this dimension. Moments in deep meditation, moments standing on a mountaintop, moments making love. But they're all just glimpses. They come and they go. Who you are is constant and eternal, but you have to be really ripe to realize this, and the ripening processes are these crises. These are what's ripening you. This is why they're happening. Be grateful for everything that happens in your life; it's all here to serve you in your awakening. Don't let your ego take over when crises happen. That's the time to keep quiet and be vigilant and let yourself ripen.

Let your suffering ripen you, so that you're ready to finish and live in the kingdom of heaven forever. Let your su-ffering become so-freeing. Embrace whatever comes your way and let it finish you. Let Existence be your Master. Whatever happens, flow with it—until you're completely living in let-go, in surrender, in trust. Let Existence ripen you. Don't hold back; don't say "no." Be available to whatever's happening in your life. Surrender, be vulnerable, open and available. Never point a finger at the Master, no matter what happens. Just look at what rises inside of you and take everything that happens as a device to finish you. No matter what rises, don't point the finger outside of yourself. Look at your own self and keep the light shining on you.

Keep the light shining on you! When the light is shining on you, everything can be seen, not just the side that you want to show to the outside world, not just your image, but all of it. Always keep the light shining on you. Don't bother looking at the other; always look at yourself. Look at your own thoughts as they arise. Look at your own stories as they arise. What you're seeing outside is nothing but a reflection of your own consciousness, so keep the light on yourself always. Instead of looking outside yourself, keep your Awareness on yourself. As soon as you see yourself misidentified, drop it. Inquire as soon as you feel somebody rise. Inquire, "Who cares? Who is this 'I'?" Let it fall away.

Once you've ripened, you fall from the tree naturally. It's a complete non-doing. In this surrender, there's nobody left to surrender. There's nobody who cares. There's nobody who wants anything. There's nobody resisting, and Existence drops you like a ripe mango! Then you're prasad for everybody: for the ants and the birds, the flies and the maggots. Let yourself ripen! Satsang is like the sun, the hot sun that's ripening you—and when you're ripe, you fall. There's nobody to let go; who's there to let go of the mango? It just lets go. When it's ripe, it lets go by itself. It only takes one moment—one moment of dropping this identification with whom you have believed yourself to be your whole life—to taste who you truly are, and your life is forever transformed.

Are you fully committed to freedom? Have you suffered enough? Are you ready to keep quiet when your mind says that you have to speak? Are you willing to do nothing when your life is telling you to keep busy, running around doing something, hoping to gain something, or hoping to experience something? Freedom happens when there is no experiencer, when there's nobody to say whether it's good or bad, when there's nobody to get in the way with silly ideas of what you believe is better or worse. There's nobody identified with duality. You must be willing to renounce everything. Everything! Not just the material, but also the conceptual—the conceptualization that you are separate. The conceptualization that you exist as form, the conceptualization that you were born and you will die. The conceptualization that you are these bodies, and all the stories that rise from that one story. You have to be willing to drop them!

Don't put conditions on yourself. Don't tell yourself to be a certain way. Love yourself. This is how it is when you're in love with the beloved, isn't it? You don't say, "I love you so much, but could you be different for me?" You only do this after you get married! You don't do this when you're in love. You accept your beloved totally, and this is how it is in freedom. You accept yourself totally. There's no more identification with the body-mind, so who cares? Then within that freedom you can play. You can adapt, you can change, you can refine. It doesn't matter. It's a painting. You add colors, you play with them, it can constantly change. But at no point do you think, "This is me," when you hold up the painting. This is just a picture of me, a symbolic representation of who I am. These bodies, these lives— you don't have to be so invested in them. This is how you live in freedom. Whatever rises falls back again, easily and effortlessly, and you just continue flowing.

If you have the good grace to come upon someone who has recognized himself as free, in that grace you recognize your Self too. All you have to do is be available. Just be available, meaning have no idea, no concept of who you believe yourself to be. Then it's contagious. Freedom is contagious! It's like a virus; it's easy to catch, but you must be defenseless! No defenses. Your ego's immune system must be completely wiped out, and then you catch it. You catch the truth. You catch the love that you are. This is your nature, so come and drop this idea of yourself and make yourself available. In this availability miracles happen! The miracle of your own Self is revealed after lifetimes of searching. We're just here to look into each other's faces in recognition. A simple recognition; that's all it takes in freedom. We look into each other's eyes and we say, "I see you. You are me. We are One." You see there's no mind to separate, no mind to push away, no mind to defend; just openness and vulnerability. This love becomes contagious, and then it happens to everyone else in the room, then everybody else in town, and then everybody else in the world. This is how it happens. It's contagious—this love, this awakening, this truth.

All of the paths, all of the traditions, and all of the practices are designed simply for you to be finished with the "I." Whether you're sitting still staring at a blank wall for ten days, or you're doing yoga for ten years, all of these practices, all of these paths are designed to assist you in dissolving the "I." The surrender to the guru is the surrender of the "I." It's the "I" who surrenders, and in that moment of surrender, it is realized that you are the guru to whom you are surrendering. Only this "I" stands in the way—this me, this ego, this one who says, "I want this and I want that." When we let go of this "I," we're in guru's grace. It can clearly be seen that everything is happening according to a divine order. You flow with this grace; you don't even have to make decisions, you simply live in choiceless Awareness. There's no need to think.

Keep your attention on nothing, on truth, on freedom, on Awareness itself. Keep your attention on the Source. Then we can soar together in satsang! At first, we soar in tandem; we fly together but don't become dependent on this form. Learn to fly on your own, so you can be in satsang all the time. You only fly tandem temporarily, and then you wake up to the truth of who you are, realizing that there's only One, and you are that One. You are the master! There is no master outside of you. You are flying now; you are always flying. Drop this mind that lives in duality: right and wrong, good and bad, worthy and unworthy, sinner and saint, lover and beloved, you and me. Drop this burden of a mind and fly unencumbered in this moment. Let yourself soar freely!

Remember there's only one of us, so in truth everyone is your master. If you make it special with one particular person, then when you're not with her what do you feel? You feel hungry, you feel lost. Love is not special; your master is everywhere. Be open and available and realize that the guru is an empty mirror. The guru is here to reflect where you are still identified, where you are still attached, where you still doubt, where you still believe, where you are still identified as somebody— especially if it is somebody special. Let the guru reflect you until you are finished with this somebody, or find another guru. Don't waste your time feeling special in a crowd full of people because he looked at you as he walked by, or she touched you with a feather, or you heard his inner voice speak to your inner voice. Use your guru as a mirror to finish with all your attachments, and surrender to Existence as it happens, because Existence is truly your master.

Freedom is your birthright. There is nothing to attain; there is nothing to get—simply be who you are. If mind rises and says you are not supposed to be who you are in this moment, do not listen! Be free! If mind rises and tells you that your partner should not be who they are in this moment, do not listen. Be free. Don't mind your mind; don't listen to it. You are free. Don't listen to your mind when it says, "No, I'm not." Don't listen to your mind when something arises, whatever it is, even the mind that says, "I am free." Do not listen to anything; just be free! Do not think about being free, and do not think about not being free. Do not think! When thoughts arise, don't pay attention to them, because this thinker is nothing but another thought. Never mind your mind, and you can be free in each and every moment.

You think you're a mind with moments of freedom, when actually you're freedom with moments of mind! This is true. You are Consciousness itself, within which thoughts are rising and falling—this is all. Whenever Consciousness identifies with a thought, it thinks that's who it is. This is the beauty of Existence! You can be anybody or anything you want to be, just by thinking of it! This is the power of imagination. But you must know it's imagination, then it's fun. You can be a variety of people in your life when you're not identified with any of it. You can have a different life each moment when you're not identified with any of it. You can be anybody in any moment. You can be the boss, or you can be the employee. You can be the parent, or you can be the child. You can be the master, or you can be the disciple. You can be the top, or you can be the bottom. You can be the first, or you can be the last. It doesn't matter; you can be anybody when you're nobody. Have the courage to be nobody! Have the courage to live in the unknown—then you're available to this moment, then you're alive in this moment, then you're not dead. Knowledge is dead. Misidentification is dead. History is dead. Somebody is dead! Don't be afraid to put an end to somebody, so that you can realize yourself as nobody! You have to be willing to let go of your misidentification as a wave before you can realize yourself as the ocean.

There appears to be an acceleration, a quickening, an availability for the truth to be realized by anyone who has a sincere and burning desire for it, anyone and everyone. You don't have to be an avatar anymore. You don't have to have three wise men show up at the hospital room where you're born! It's available to everyone, this realization, the truth of who we are. All it takes is a burning desire, a really strong desire for this realization. It has to be more powerful, more prominent than any other desire you have. If your commitment to freedom is your top priority, if your abidance in silence, in love, in God-Consciousness is all that interests you, then it is inevitable that the truth will find you. You will not have to realize truth; truth will realize you! Freedom will overcome you, because this "you" will no longer be interested in running from it, avoiding it, and missing it by seeking something else. By not seeking anything else, the seeker falls away. All external objects fall away and the internal subject that you are, the pure, potent Awareness that you are, is all that remains.

This silent celebration is catching fire. Many, many people just like yourself are waking up to this truth. Recognize this now: you are home free. The powerful realization of the ordinariness of enlightenment will revolutionize this world. It is so radical, because it doesn't come from thought; it doesn't come from concept; it doesn't change an idea, or recondition a mind. It's a radical dropping of mind, of all ideas. You are revolutionaries of truth! Recognize this and live this truth in your daily life. This is how the world that you live in changes. It changes on the unconscious level. As you change, your world changes. Be radical! It's a revolution from within. Stop trying to change the outer. Stop wasting your time and make the shift now. Everything you need is available to you. You are the Source. Join this revolution! Free yourself from any concept that freedom is in the future. Wake up right now and live in this freedom. No more postponement. No more excuses. No more stories. It just takes a willingness to realize that you are the unknown, the unconscious, the unmanifest, pure and innocent, untouched by mind, untouched by concept. You are freedom itself!

Are you ready to stop searching for God and see the God that you are? Are you ready to stop chasing happiness and be happiness itself? Are you ready to stop looking for love and realize yourself as love? Are you ready to come out of the closet as God? In truth, no one comes out of the closet. The closet simply disappears, and you're exposed—because there's no more defense, there's no more thinking about it. There's just the pure presence of your Awareness in this moment. There's no more need to hide out. If enough of us wake up, they can't crucify us all! Come on, come out of the closet as God! Realize there's only one of us, and this One is wide awake.

The Master Peace

You are already perfect just the way you are.
Don't touch anything.
Don't make any more effort.
Don't spoil the magnificent painting that you are.
Just leave it be.
It's perfect just the way it is,
This painting, this masterpiece.
You are a master and you are peace itself.
You are the Master Peace.
This is what you have come to recognize.
You are already whatever it is
You have been seeking your whole life.
Whatever this ideal has been,
Whatever symbol you have placed on it,
Be it Love or Success or Happiness,
Peace or Freedom or Enlightenment.
You are already That.
This is the Truth, I promise you.
This is the Truth.

Prasad offers public Satsang, weekend intensives
and week-long retreats.
For further information regarding his schedule,
or to order books, videos, audio tapes and CD's,
please call the Prasad Foundation at 1-800-242-0363 ext. 2753
or visit www.prasadsatsang.com